A PRINCIPAL'S TALE

A PRINCIPAL'S TALE

A SELF-DETERMINED LEADER

SHELLEY MCINTOSH ED.D

J. Merrill
PUBLISHING

J Merrill Publishing, Inc., Columbus 43207
www.JMerrillPublishingInc.com

Library of Congress Control Number: 2020923578
ISBN-13: 978-1-950719-66-2 (Paperback)
ISBN-13: 978-1-950719-65-5 (eBook)

Title: A Principal's Tale
Author: Shelley McIntosh, Ed.D.
Cover Artwork: Deon Yates

CONTENTS

Acknowledgments   vii

Prologue   ix

Reality 1 – How Can the Cafeteria Be Orderly?   1

Reality 2 – How to Organize Student Activities   5

Reality 3 – Who Really Is the Principal?   9

Reality 4 – Bullying Is Not Allowed Here!   13

Reality 5 – Students Meet School Leadership   17

Reality 6 – My Administrative Assistant Saved My Life   21

Reality 7 – New Teacher Orientation   25

Reality 8 – Calming the Storm of Overlapping Responsibilities   29

Reality 9 – Curtailing Early Student Pickup   31

Reality 10 – Why Is This Student Late?   33

Reality 11 – Teacher Evaluations   35

Reality 12 – A Kindergarten Runner   37

Reality 13 – Combing Hair?   39

Reality 14 – Gossip, Take It to the Source   41

Reality 15 – Valuing Students   45

Reality 16 – Who Is the Staff?   47

Reality 17 – Faculty Meetings   49

Reality 18 – Black History Month   57

Reality 19 – Administrative Team and Its Importance   67

Reality 20 – Teacher Leadership Team   71

Reality 21 – Positive Environment for Teachers   75

Reality 22 – Fulfilling Teachers' Needs for Resources   79

Reality 23 – Instituting Yoga and Meditation   81

Reality 24 – The Literacy Dilemma   83

Reality 25 – The Principal's Glass House   87

Reality 26 – Boys and Girls Learn Differently   89
Reality 27 – Culturally Responsive Teaching   93

Epilogue   97
Also by Shelley McIntosh Ed.D   101

ACKNOWLEDGMENTS

In education, all is done for the benefit of the child. This requires a vision and mission that take into account the total environment created by administrators, teachers, and parents. I am grateful for all.

Administrators are leaders whose primary responsibility is to provide leadership and to influence others in positive ways. My gratitude to Solid Rock Management Company for its impactful leadership; and the administrators in the Winans' district, Dr. Haywood, Dr. Godine, Mrs. Abbott, Dr. Ponder, and Mr. Pettway.

Teachers have the most significant impact on student learning. The power of their roles create futures for children. I appreciate the commitment, flexibility, professionalism, and creativity exhibited by teachers at Marvin L. Winans Academy of Performing Arts, elementary school.

I believe that most parents desire for their children to live a life of happiness, health, prosperity, and accomplishments. It was their choice to trust the school with their children's lives. To all the parents who volunteered, chaperoned, participated in meetings, and voiced your concerns, I honor and give ultimate respect. Thank you.

Janina Lawrence, I am grateful for your tedious editing to make my passion a coherent and informative read.

Jackie Smith, Jr. of J Merrill Publishing, our paths crossed, and I am so glad they did. Your professionalism and friendliness made the publishing journey doable and rewarding.

> "It is easier to build strong children than to repair broken men."
>
> – Frederick Douglass

PROLOGUE

WHERE I'M FROM

My DNA says I'm from the Congo,
Ghana, Togo,
Senegal, and
Nigeria.
From ancestors I can only imagine through my
mind's depictions.
I'm from the institution of slavery and
freed grandparents.
I'm from the Reverend Rufus James Miller and
Rutha Lee Craig,
Parents of the Black Migration from south to
north in America.
They traveled all the way with a baby girl,
the twin that survived
and made the city of Detroit their new home
where they welcomed
their third daughter, first to be born up north,

Shelley Elaine.
I'm from being educated in Detroit schools,
ranked tenth in class.
I'm from the swinging melodies of Motown
Flowing, flowing,
Penetrating our eastside neighborhood
Life was so good!
I'm from civil rights, rebellions, and social
justice afro.
Community was the theory and practice
Serve without pay
"Momma, you mean I can't get minimum wage?
I babysat all day."
I'm from service and leadership
nationally directing youth programs
supervising student teachers,
ministering christening and marriages
leading adults and children's groups.
I'm from higher education, teaching undergrad and
grad courses, serving on numerous committees,
and writing scholarly papers.
I'm from being an urban school principal with an
unrelenting passion that everything is done for
the benefit of the child.
I'm from Education Chose Me.

I place myself in context to better know myself. Providing a context allows me to see the bigger picture. The old adage, "You can't see the forest for the trees," simply meaning that focusing on one tree narrows vision or perspective. Focusing on the forest, we see that the tree belongs to a family of trees and that beauty abounds. It is a resting place and playground for birds, food for animals. The forest roots run deep. One purpose of the forest is to transform our exhale of carbon dioxide into our inhale of oxygen to support our lives.

To understand urban school administration and self-determination theory, everything must be put into context so the context, *forest,* what motivates human beings, and the context, *forest*, of urban school principals.

In schools, principals and teachers struggle with how to motivate those that they serve: students, parents, and oftentimes themselves. Motivation is defined as moving ourselves or others to act. What is it that motivates us?

As a principal, I believed that my service would make a difference in the lives of students. This motivated me to arise every morning at 5 a.m. and travel at least twenty-six miles to school, a thirty-minute drive in every season—sunny summer, blossoming spring, beautiful fall, and frigid winter. I was also confident that serving as a teacher, earning a master's and a doctorate in curriculum and instruction, and gaining leadership skills as a church administrator and group leader for over twenty-five years, created a high level of competence both in organizational and social skills. Accordingly, the management company allowed room for autonomous decisions, such as creating an All Dads Club, designing banners for school-wide cleanup and appropriate cafeteria behaviors, developing teams, and implementing classroom meetings. As with many principals, I was highly motivated, not solely for the salary but for the differences we could make in children's lives. The research of Edward Deci and Richard Ryan, psychologists at the University of Rochester, expanded my knowledge base, understanding, and awareness of motivation.

SELF-DETERMINATION THEORY

Self-determination theory - Basic Psychological Needs Theory (BPNT) posits that all human beings are active organisms, with evolved tendencies toward growing, mastering challenges, and integrating new experiences into a coherent sense of self.

Self-determination theory identifies three psychological needs that, when met internally, motivates one to act: the need for autonomy, the need for competence, and the need for relatedness.

Autonomy is defined as independence in one's thoughts or actions; behaving with a sense of using one's own will, willingness, and choice. It is not controlled by someone pressuring you to do something or separable rewards. Example: A teacher deciding to attend a professional development session of her choice.

Competence means the ability to do something successfully or efficiently; mastering one's environment. Example: A baby learning to walk needs no formal class. Starting the process by lifting his head, rolling over, rocking on hands and knees, he prepares to crawl or roll. Then pulling himself up, holding on to a chair, and holding parents' hands, the baby finally masters the difficult art of walking - balancing and moving while one foot is on the ground and the other is off.

Relatedness is connectedness to others, a feeling of being related to others, a sense of belonging, caring for others, and being cared for, according to Gagné and Deci. Examples: A student feeling that a teacher cares benefits the student in feeling motivated to engage and learn. Also, positive relationships between students and teachers create a sense of belonging. Teachers who feel accepted by colleagues and administration feel supported.

These natural developmental tendencies require ongoing social supports. That means others' behaviors can either support or prevent the natural tendencies for active engagement and psychological growth. If needs are met, a person becomes self-determined or self-motivated. What does this support look like? Deci and Flaste illustrate this in the following quote:

"If you put an avocado pit in a pot of earth it will probably grow into a tree, because it is in the nature of avocados to do that... [But for that to occur] they need sun; they need water, and they need the right temperatures. Those elements do not make trees grow, but they are the nutriments that the developing avocados need, that are necessary in order for the avocados to do what they do naturally."

Similarly, when a baby is born to caring parents, their body will grow and develop in stages to adulthood because it is in the nature of the human body to do that. So nutriments of food, air, and water are needed for the baby's body to do what it does naturally; to grow and transform itself. Moreover, for the baby's healthy, psychological growth, the environment must be a supportive one.

A nurturing environment feeds the psychological needs for competence, autonomy, and relatedness resulting in well-being, satisfaction, happiness, and mental and emotional health. For example, a kindergarten teacher is acutely aware that her five-year-old students are learning how to write their names. She notices that they need support. So, she painstakingly writes dotted letters for each student's names so they can trace them. She teaches how to hold a pencil, then checks each student gently repositioning their small fingers. In addition, she explains and models how to trace the letters—at times, placing her hand over the hand of the student to guide his tracing. Providing encouraging praise and practice, students work hard and get better. This teacher, in fact, nurtures, supports and uplifts students to be competent.

In contrast, an environment that is not nurturing creates psychological and social problems, such as depression, guilt, shame, anger, frustration, low self-esteem, and narcissism. A kindergarten teacher complains that her five-year-old students cannot write their names yet. She adamantly declares that parents should have done a better job and implies that they are negligent. In essence, she blames the parents. Through tone of voice and words, she imparts the message that students should know how to do this by now. Or, she may provide students with writing worksheets, but fails to model how to hold a pencil and how to write letters. She may bombard students verbally. Such as, "you didn't write that correctly. Really, you should remember; we did this last week. You are lazy and didn't pay attention." This environment is not nurturing. Children are discouraged, demeaned, and feel incompetent.

Self-determination theory provides the basis for urban school principals to ask a critical question. Are the psychological needs of autonomy, competence, and relatedness being met in my school so that teachers, students, parents, and even I am self-motivated or self-determined? When urban school administrators look through the lens of the self-determination theory, they observe with clarity what nurtures and what oppresses competence, autonomy, and relatedness.

First, some characteristics of the urban, inner-city school are listed below:

- More likely to serve low-income students where more than 40 percent of students receive free or reduced lunch.
- On average, students attending urban, inner-city schools have lower achievement scores in reading, writing, math, and science.
- There tends to be more problems in behavior, absenteeism, and classroom discipline; children are less likely to feel safe and are less likely to spend much time on homework.
- Urban teachers have fewer resources available to them and less control over their curriculum than teachers in other areas; they also have overcrowded classrooms.
- Finally, urban schools have more teachers and instructors teaching out of their content areas.

Why and How is this the state of urban schools? Renowned author, Jonathan Kozol, documents the reasons in his books entitled *Savage Inequalities* (1991) and *The Shame of a Nation* (2005). The reasons he cited still currently exist. Some glaring social oppressive measures are inequality, joblessness, and poverty. Urban school principals, looking through the lens of the self-determination theory, become knowledgeable about the educational bureaucracy beginning with state government. The following observations (one through five) viewed through the lens of the self-determination theory allow urban school principals to be analytical, critical, and self-reflective.

Observation 1

The public school system is owned and operated by the government. Each state's legislators are responsible for overseeing and ruling on decisions involving public schools in that state. States are primarily responsible for the maintenance and operation of public schools. They are heavily involved in the establishment, selection, and regulation of curriculum, teaching methods, and instructional materials in their schools.

As indicated in the Michigan Senate Fiscal Agency Report of 2018-2019, funding of schools is based on a foundation allowance, which is a dollar amount allotted per student. It has also been determined that at least $10,000 is needed per student each year to educate them properly. The lowest-funded schools are in the Detroit Public School Community District, rural districts, and include charter schools with a student allowance of $7,871. The highest-funded schools, primarily located in suburbs of Detroit, Michigan, such as Birmingham, Bloomfield, and Farmington Hills, receive $12,244 per student. Overall, approximately 84 percent of districts receive the lowest funding compared to 16 percent, which receives above the minimum.

In calculating the math, a school in West Bloomfield with 700 students will receive $8,570,800. A school in the inner city, for example, the charter school where I served as principal with 700 students, received $5,509,700—a $3 million difference. But, we both need the same number of teachers, must pay for textbooks, administrator and teacher salaries, school furniture, office personnel, instructional materials, and maintenance. That's why on Count Days, inner-city schools organize parties, with special snacks and treats, because if students are absent, it could result in a loss of funds that equal a teacher's salary; therefore, a loss of a teacher or a school's inability to hire the number of teachers needed.

Observation 2

Michigan state legislators proposed the third-grade reading standard, which was signed into law in 2016. This law has been adopted in several states and requires that a third-grade student be retained if he or she tests more than two grade levels behind on the state's student assessment. It makes me wonder if this conversation occurred at the Mackinac Island Summit between a businessman of a multimillion-dollar test-taking corporation and a state legislator as they shared a cocktail. Why punish students? Kozol writes in *The Shame of the Nation* that under the guise of school reform, there is a relentless emphasis on raising test scores and rigid policies of non-promotion and non-graduation.

Observation 3

Michigan is one of the four most segregated states for Black students. In *The Shame of a Nation*, Kozol refers to these schools as Apartheid Schools because the student population is 99 percent to 100 percent African American (2005).

Observation 4

The Detroit Public School Community is the district governing Detroit schools and derives its power and authority from the state. The purpose of the elected school board is to serve as the governing body of the district and to provide education services to children residing within the geographic boundaries of the city of Detroit. The board sees that schools are operated properly, but do not administer them directly; administration is the job of the superintendent. The most important responsibility of the school board is to work with their communities to improve student achievement in their local public schools.

Yet, Michigan is the worst state for teaching Black boys to read and the second-worst to teach White boys to read. It is one of the lowest literacy states, as reported by the National Assessment of Educational Progress (NAEP). Alarmingly, the majority of students in the city of Detroit are still below grade level in reading. In addition, Detroit's child poverty rate is at about 48 percent, that is almost half of the children as reported in *AP News* -

September 2018): "Detroit Income Rises, Poverty Rate Doesn't Improve."

Observation 5

School principals are licensed/certified by the state. The overall responsibility is to promote the success of all students. The Interstate School Leaders Licensure Consortium (ISLLC) provides six standards that address a principal's need to promote the success of all students.

Standard 1: A school administrator is an educational leader who promotes the success of all students by facilitating the development, articulation, implementation, and stewardship of a vision of learning that is shared and supported by the school community.

Standard 2: A school administrator is an educational leader who promotes the success of all students by advocating, nurturing, and sustaining the school culture and instructional program conducive to learning and staff professional development.

Standard 3: A school administrator is an educational leader who promotes the success of all students by ensuring management of the organization, operations, and resources for a safe, efficient, and effective learning environment.

Standard 4: A school administrator is an educational leader who promotes the success of all students by collaborating with families and community members, responding to diverse community interests and needs, and mobilizing community resources.

Standard 5: A school administrator is an educational leader who promotes the success of all students by acting with integrity, fairness, and in an ethical manner.

Standard 6: A school administrator is an educational leader who promotes the success of all students by understanding, responding to, and influencing the larger political, social, economic, legal, and cultural context.

Yet, Kate Rousmaniere, a professor at Miami University, wrote an article entitled, "The Principal: The Most Misunderstood Person in

All of Education." She explains that principals serve as middle managers (based on a business model) located between the school and the district, and serving both. They are hired to promote large-scale initiatives and to solve immediate day-to-day problems, carrying multiple, and often contradictory, responsibilities. She quotes sociologist C. Wright Mills, "Principals are in white-collar positions, 'the assistants of authority' whose power was derived from others to implement managerial decisions but had limited opportunities for influencing those decisions." This poses a major dilemma for urban school principals whose job is a middle manager between directives issued by the district (influenced by state legislators) and the real needs of their teachers, students, parents, and communities.

In all five observations, an urban school principal needs to identify what nurtures and what oppresses competence, autonomy, and relatedness in his/her school community. What hinders the natural tendency to be self-determined, to be self-motivated?

Does one choose the role of compliance boss or a leader that influences? How does a principal navigate the middle manager position? The five observations viewed through the lens of the self-determination theory reflect the forest of education and, more importantly, the need for a supportive social environment.

When urban school administrators look through the lens of the self-determination theory, they see with clearer vision what nurtures and what oppresses competence, autonomy, and relatedness.

MY EYEWITNESS STORY

My mother and father were part of the last Black Migration from a segregated, discriminatory, unjust South to hopes of opportunity in the North. Analyzing the big picture, this was the period of the industrialization of cars, and Black labor was needed. I can only imagine how they traveled with a small child, my oldest sister, to start a whole new life without enough resources. My father served in the army during World War II, and I remember him coming home in his uniform with puzzles of the United States. I remember living on the west side, on McGraw Street, and then with my aunt on Floyd Street. We moved to the east side in an old, two-family flat on Fisher that was infested with roaches and rats, which my father fought through fumigation, setting rat traps, and sealing rat holes with aluminum. I don't recall when he started working at the Chrysler Plant on Jefferson, but I remember him catching the bus every day. About sixteen years after I was born, he was able to afford a car. I was unaware that certain laws were oppressive and racially motivated. These laws favored White families by providing subsidized mortgage loans to move into the suburbs, confining Black families to designated areas and zip codes, and denying mortgage loans to Black people. Many laws are intended to control and oppress Black people as well as to maintain racial separation. This included my father.

I attended Scripps Elementary School, Foch Middle School, and Southeastern High School. For one year, I was bused to A.L. Holmes. (I didn't know busing was required to desegregate schools; I was only in the seventh grade). Because many unskilled Black men found work in car factories, they were able to provide food, shelter, and clothing for their families. My father worked at Chrysler for thirty-three years. It was a better Detroit, a friendlier Bewick Street, because of the growing Black middle class. Neighbors knew each other, children walked to and from schools, and businesses flourished on Mack Street. Motown hit the scene, and we felt like a community. But, Black people, especially Black men, were being harassed by the police, called the Big Four.

In 1967, Black people rebelled against constant police brutality sparked by a police raid on an unlicensed bar, known locally as a "blind pig." On July 23rd, the vice squad of the mostly White Detroit Police Department raided the bar located on 12th Street and Clairmount. Twelfth Street was the epicenter of Black retail. Dozens of partygoers were arrested. A stone was thrown and shattered the window of a police cruiser, starting a rash of break-ins, burglaries, and arson. The crisis resulted in forty-three deaths, hundreds of injuries, approximately seventeen hundred fires, and over seven thousand arrests. The Detroit Rebellion of 1967 and the 12th Street Riot is known as the largest civil disturbance of twentieth-century America culminated because of decades of institutional racism and entrenched segregation. I lived on the eastside, and the spirit of the rebellion spread. Businesses were set on fire —almost all of them on Mack Street, a thriving business center. I was still in high school and unaware that the Michigan State Police and the U.S. Army were involved in quelling the disturbance. However, I was keenly aware of the National Guard because they set up headquarters at my high school. The city was on lockdown, schools were closed, and a 9 p.m. curfew was set for the entire city to be indoors. I heard the National Guard marching, crooning military calls, and patrolling our neighborhood morning and night.

After the rebellion, drugs were pumped into the Black community with the intent to pacify and quench the uprising revolutionary spirit of a people. Because of a major shift in the U.S. economy to an informational and computerized era, there was a decline in manufacturing jobs. Many unskilled Black men, now jobless, began selling drugs, destroying other lives for the sake of their own survival. When the social environment prevents the needs of competence, autonomy, and connectedness, serious psychological problems emerge, including self-destructive tendencies.

Coleman Young was elected in 1974 as the first Black mayor of Detroit. He walked into the office at a time when White businesses decided not to invest in the city. Joblessness was increasing, and property taxes, a major funding for schools, was decreasing. Without jobs, without monetary resources, and with racist laws, POVERTY increased. LACK OF RESOURCES was prominent. These conditions thwart the innate needs to be competent, to be autonomous, to relate, and to be self-determined.

Principals, teachers, and parents also can thwart or oppress the need to be self-determined.

Principals can oppress teachers by not seriously assessing the curriculum load, by disrespectful language, and by disregarding teachers' voices.

Teachers can oppress students by labeling them as lazy, by using demeaning comments, and by not providing adequate support.

Parents can oppress children by threatening them, using profanity, and abusing them.

Students can oppress one another by bullying and name-calling. So, with these odds, is it possible to create an environment that nurtures competence, autonomy, and relatedness?

I served as principal of the Marvin L. Winans Academy of Performing Arts for six years. It was located on the east side of Detroit. Historically, many African Americans settled in this area during the Black Migrations. The community had been in transition, moving from jobs to joblessness, from homeowners to renters, and from incomes to lower incomes. Yet, the school serves as a haven for many well-deserving children. It is one of the most unique schools in the greater metropolitan area because of its extraordinary performing arts programs from kindergarten through the twelfth grade.

The first edition of a *Principal's Tale: Life in 31 Days* chronicled my life as an administrator in the format of a daily journal and reflections. My purpose was to paint a vivid picture of the myriad experiences being an administrator without reference to any theory. In this edition of *A Principal's Tale: A Self-Determined Leader,* I present the realities and resolutions I addressed during my tenure as principal. However, this book reflects on self-determination theory and intrinsic motivation. Realities are organized by topics, each with a reflection and a reflection question.

It is with great anticipation that my written word provides a glimpse into my mode of operation, organization, and commitment to the education of children. Hopefully, it adds to the knowledge base of administrators and compliments their work and resolutions. Additionally, I seek to share my unrelenting passion, movement of inner energy that motivates me to create a culture that nurtures the competence, autonomy, and relatedness of all in the school community.

*D*on't change anything the first year as a principal in an already-established school. Spend the first year learning about the culture, personnel, and operations. This advice was given to me by a colleague. So, I embraced it. About three weeks before I began my first day, I met with various entities to get a broad picture of perceived challenges and issues. These entities were office and food personnel, paraprofessionals, and teachers. During the meeting in my office with the fourteen paraprofessionals, I asked, "What are some of your concerns?"

"The cafeteria!"

"Please explain."

"One major issue is the unruly behavior of students in the cafeteria, and the other is teachers returning late from lunch to pick up their classes. Since we supervise lunchtime often, we need help," they voiced passionately.

Others also voiced the cafeteria concern. But, in addition, complaints were made about the use of microwaves and small refrigerators in the classrooms. I gave these concerns serious thought. Do we want the aroma of popcorn and frozen steak dinners permeating the classrooms and hallways? Do we want students handling microwaves? How do you maintain stimulating classrooms for students? How is a school orderly and safe if the cafeteria is not? After discussing these with the assistant principal, Dr. Goodman, I decided that some changes needed to be made, even though I was in my first year as a principal. Changes were absolutely necessary!

~

RESOLUTION 1

I took the risk of asking teachers to eat lunch with their classes during the first semester from September through December. I know that private lunchtimes are due to teachers. At a faculty meeting before the first day of school, I explained the situation.

"We are required to provide a safe and orderly school, not only in classrooms but also in hallways and the cafeteria. We are facing unruly student behavior at lunchtime. In an effort to create a safe and orderly school throughout, I am asking you to eat with your classes for only one semester."

Yes, I got some pushback and grumbling. "We have to walk too far to the teachers' lounge to use the microwave." "We were always able to have microwaves." "I use mine to make coffee." My response, "Yes, I know, but the objective is to create a learning environment, not one of leisure." To soothe the need for coffee, I requested that the food service team prepare coffee and tea each morning. Teachers could stop by the cafeteria and help themselves.

Teachers did eat with their classes. Dr. Goodman, assistant principal, and I often ate in the cafeteria if we weren't required to attend meetings or address pressing issues. After the first semester, teachers were relieved, and Ms. Green, a second-grade teacher, later told me, "You did keep your promise, and I appreciate that."

～

REFLECTION:

Risk-taking is an individual, autonomous endeavor; however, in the school environment, it involves other individuals as well.

～

REFLECTION QUESTION:

What is your perception of autonomy?

REALITY 2 – HOW TO ORGANIZE STUDENT ACTIVITIES

*W*ithin the school community, student activities are major. Honoring students is foundational to their sense of accomplishment and their self-esteem. Activities that I reference are the: (1) spelling bee, (2) science fair, (3) fifth-grade promotion ceremony, (4) Moving Up Day, and (5) honor assemblies. Needless to say, the organization of each is critical.

The spelling bee requires that a schedule is devised that coincides with the local and national dates. Study word lists need to be distributed; each class must have their own spelling contests to determine which student qualifies to participate in the school's spelling bee; a schedule for kindergarten through grade two spelling bee must be created; a schedule for grades three through five spelling bee must be created; assignment of teachers and staff to conduct the spelling bee must be managed; readjustment of the school's regular schedule needs to be coordinated, setup of the location needs to be planned with tables, chairs, and microphones, and medals for first, second, and third place winners.

The science fair requires just as much detailed organization. Science exhibit guidelines must be distributed to teachers, display boards purchased, a parent information meeting scheduled, solicitation of judges completed, location for viewing identified, table cloths purchased, tables set up, refreshments for judges set out, and rubrics to assess science fair entries determined.

The fifth-grade promotion required preparing a format, printing programs, inviting a guest speaker, collaborating with the performing arts team for performances, fifth-grade practice of processional and song, parent invitations, and refreshments.

Moving Up Day was suggested by a kindergarten teacher, Mrs. Markle. The purpose was for students to experience the classroom of their next grade. The organization for this included mechanics of how students would move to the next grade teacher, explicit instructions to teachers regarding times and activities, contacting the middle school principal to prepare for fifth graders, and reserving buses for transportation.

Honor assemblies are scheduled to honor students in attendance, citizenship, and scholarship. Categories of academic success include the Chancellor's List, Principal's List, and Honor Roll. Coordinating these required collaborating with teachers to identify students, facilitating two honor assemblies, one for kindergarten through second grade and the other third through fifth grade. It also involved invitations to parents and preparation of certificates. I questioned myself about how these could be done effectively.

∾

RESOLUTION 2

Teachers are creative and possess great organizational skills. To tap in on these qualities for student activities, I set up teacher-led committees. At the beginning of each new school year, specifically the two weeks prior to the first day, my administrative assistant prepared signup sheets for each committee. Teachers could sign up as a committee chair or as a member. This worked well for the most part. Sometimes, I had to recruit a chair. I met with chairpersons to review responsibilities and to discuss their plans. Since service to the school is included as one component of the teacher evaluation tool, serving on a committee could satisfy it. Figure 1 identifies these professional committees.

Figure 1: Professional Committees

Committees are organized around school-related tasks and events. A chair can volunteer, be designated by the principal, or selected by the committee. In lieu of a chair, a committee member must chair the first meeting. All committees must have at least one parent as a member. Serving on a committee constitutes service beyond teaching.

Moving Up Day Committee
(Students experience their next grade up)

Grandparents' Day and Founder's Day Committee
(Appreciation for grandparents as caretakers; honoring the founder)

Interior Beautification Committee
(Keeping teacher's lounge, hallways, common areas presentable)

Parents' Center
(Develop the center following a parent-centered model)

Spelling Bee Committee/Quiz Bowl
(Organize both events)

Honors Assembly
(Organize all activities)

Science Fair Committee
(Organize all activities)

Café Planning Committee
(Plan for a well-organized, self-disciplined lunchroom)

Curriculum Committee
(Develop, organize, evaluate, promote school's curriculum)

∼

REFLECTION: Relationships, relationships, relationships are the threads that connect people to common goals and motivate them to act.

~

REFLECTION QUESTION: How are various student activities organized in your school community?

Reality 3 – Who Really Is the Principal?

*U*pon asking a first-grade male student who was the principal, he said, "Mr. Hinkle," who is not the principal but is the dean of students. Why would he give that answer when I, Dr. McIntosh, is the principal? Maybe, it's because he got in trouble and he saw the dean of students. Perhaps, he sees Mr. Hinkle in the cafeteria, the hallways, or in the parking lot directing traffic. Nevertheless, he didn't know who the principal was. I believe it is important that students know who fills that position and what the position requires. After some thought and discussion, I decided on the following.

Resolution 3

Although parents and students are required to attend an orientation where the principal is introduced, and school information is provided, some students still fail to remember. So, I planned for students to hear my voice each morning over the public announcement system. Not only will they hear it, but they will also hear character-building messages daily. An example is below. Entitled, "Whose School Is It Anyway? (Zoom, Zip, Zap is an initiative that involves students in keeping a clean school. Saints is the school name for students).

Whose school is it anyway?

All Saints should say, "It is our school."

That is why we Zoom, Zip, Zap.

That is why we remove our caps.

That is why we stand quiet in line.

That is why we are on time!

Whose school is it anyway?

All Saints should say, "It is our school."

That is why we use quiet voices.

That is why we make the right choices.

That is why we are polite.

That is why we don't fight.

Whose school is it anyway?

All Saints should say, "It is our school!"

That was the first line of attack.

The second was to visit classrooms and introduce myself. I conferenced with my administrative assistant, Mrs. Burrough, to inform teachers that I would make a brief stop in their classrooms, including the date and time. My first stop was a third-grade classroom. As I entered, Mrs. Turner announced, "Saints, our principal is here to visit us." As I moved to a chair at the front of the class, I began.

"Good Morning, Mrs. Turner and Saints."

"Good Morning, Dr. McIntosh, we are blessed to be in your presence."

"I am blessed to be in your presence. Most of you know that my name is Dr. McIntosh. Why do they call me a doctor?"

A brown-skinned boy wearing glasses and named Jaden replied, "Maybe, you make people well."

Smiling, I quickly responded, "Not quite."

"I was in the third grade just like you, but I grew up. I graduated from high school and went to college for five years to earn my bachelor's degree. That is the first degree." I put up five fingers.

"Then, I went another two years to get a master's degree." I put up seven fingers.

"I finally went three more years to get a doctorate degree, which is the highest you can get in a university." I put up ten fingers. "How long did I go to college?" Students shouted, "Ten years!"

"But guess what? I am always learning," I continued.

"I am your principal, which means that I am the main one responsible for what goes on in the school. I have two children, but they are all grown up, and I have four grandchildren. Are there any questions you want to ask me?"

The questions came one after the other: "How old are you?" "Where do you live?" "Do you like being a principal?" "Where is your mom and dad?"

My answers: "I am much older than you are." "I live in Farmington Hills." "I love being your principal." "My mom and dad passed away."

Immediately dozens of hands were raised—student after student had something to say.

"My uncle died."

"My grandmother died, and I miss her."

"My cousin was shot and killed."

My sole statement that my parents had passed tapped students' memories of loved ones they had lost. It seemed to me that a safe door, unbeknownst to me, was now open for them to share their experiences. They were only eight-year-olds! The best that I could do was listen. Then, I attempted to console them with words to remember the good times they shared with their loved ones, ending with a moment of silence.

The purpose of getting to know the principal was for relationship and connection, but it also allowed me to know my students. I visited about ten classrooms out of thirty at the onset, but I must admit my schedule was inundated with many other responsibilities, so I did not complete it. However, I made my presence known in each class so that they could say Dr. McIntosh is the principal with total confidence.

∽

REFLECTION: When all layers are peeled away, we are all living organisms desiring to connect through our stories.

∽

REFLECTION QUESTION: What is your story for the many hats you wear?

REALITY 4 – BULLYING IS NOT ALLOWED HERE!

*B*ullying is unwanted, aggressive behavior among school-aged children and adults, which involves a real or perceived power imbalance. The behavior is repeated or has the potential to be repeated over time. Both kids who are bullied and who bully others may have serious, lasting problems.

In order to be considered bullying, the behavior must be aggressive and include:

An Imbalance of Power: Kids who bully use their power—such as physical strength, access to embarrassing information, or popularity—to control or harm others. Power imbalances can change over time and in different situations, even if they involve the same people.

Repetition: Bullying behaviors happen more than once or have the potential to happen more than once.

Bullying includes making threats, spreading rumors, attacking someone physically or verbally, and excluding someone from a group on purpose.

TYPES OF BULLYING

There are three types of bullying:

Verbal bullying is saying or writing hurtful things. Verbal bullying includes:

- Teasing
- Name-calling
- Inappropriate sexual comments

- Taunting
- Threatening to cause harm

Social bullying, sometimes referred to as relational bullying, involves hurting someone's reputation or relationships. Social bullying includes:

- Leaving someone out on purpose
- Telling other children not to be friends with someone
- Spreading rumors about someone
- Embarrassing someone in public

Physical bullying involves hurting a person's body or possessions. Physical bullying includes:

- Hitting/kicking/pinching
- Spitting
- Tripping/pushing
- Taking or breaking someone's things
- Making hurtful or rude hand gestures

~

RESOLUTION 4

The school policy has zero-tolerance for bullying. Consequences include suspension and possible expulsion. I had an idea to address bullying classroom by classroom. With my administration, I discussed Bully Round-Up Day. Each member of the administration team would dress in all black so that students would perceive the formidable power, authority, and seriousness of bullying. (Students probably didn't think we were that formidable, but we tried!). The plan: Divide into two groups. Enter the classroom. Announce who we are and give a short talk about bullying. Ask the class who has been bullied. So, on Bully Round-Up Day, we began our mission in the five second-grade classrooms. First, the five-person administration team entered one classroom. I explained various types of bullying. Then, I asked who were the bullies in the classroom. The classmates identified two or three students as bullies. We beckoned them to come to the front of the room and stand in line. Other students raised their hands, pointing out two or three additional bullies. The alleged bullies then pointed their fingers at the accusers. What started as three now quickly escalated to ten. My quiet but desperate reflection caused me to silently say to myself, "This is bigger than I anticipated." But the mission, although partially accepted, had to be continued.

The alleged bullies were marched to the main hallway with the administrative team admonishing them to stay in a straight line. I figured that we were in that classroom too long, so I recommended that two of the administrative team go into one room and the other three in the next one. Much to our dismay, about thirty bullies had been identified and were now lined up in the main hallway. I said to myself, "This will be the first and last time doing this, but we must complete the mission."

The administrative team dressed in all black (fantasizing *The Men in Black*), guided this long line of students to the library, instructed them to sit in rows on the carpet, and lectured them on ways to treat other students: (1) If you get angry, step back from your classmate. (2) Take ten deep breaths. (3) Walk away. (4) Do not hit first. (5) Call your classmates by the names their parents gave them. (6) You can use endearing terms for your classmates, such as "Sugar Bear, Honey Bun, Jelly Bean." (7) Report the incident to your teacher. We modeled and then instructed students to practice the steps. In addition, I explained how each student is connected and belongs to a mother, father, sister, brother, cousin, and that when they bully a classmate, everyone in the family is affected.

After twenty minutes of lecture and practice, we escorted students back to their classrooms with the realization that this mission will be aborted; however, significant learning did take place about what to do when angry or bullied. It was reinforced by an affirmation I created for the students entitled "Buddies not Bullies."

Buddies love.
Bullies shove.
Buddies are kind.
Bullies pay no mind.
Buddies say, "Hi."
Bullies make others cry.
Buddies help everyone.
Bullies help no one.
Buddies love to make others smile.
Bullies make people sad for a while.
Buddies keep a clean school.
Bullies break all the rules.
Buddies learn to be all they can be.
Bullies only study a little, you see.

Who are the best? WAPA Buddies
Who are the best? WAPA Buddies
Who are the best? WAPA Buddies
(WAPA–Winans Academy of Performing Arts)

~

REFLECTION: An African proverb states that it is the responsibility of the community to shape and mold the child. So then, the behaviors of children are a reflection of how good a job the community is doing.

~

REFLECTION QUESTION: What are ways to transform student behaviors?

REALITY 5 – STUDENTS MEET SCHOOL LEADERSHIP

*T*here are many perspectives that students and faculty have about administration. From students believing the principal's office is where you go when you get in trouble to teachers perceiving the situation from a "them" and "us" perspective. "Them" is the principal and administration team. "Us" constitutes the teaching staff. Knowing the stories and backgrounds help to bridge the gap.

~

RESOLUTION 5

I decided that a whole school assembly would be held with the theme of "To Be Young, Gifted, and Black." I discussed the idea with my administrative team, which consisted of the assistant principal, the coordinator of special education, the curriculum specialist, and the dean of students. Within our discussion, I expressed the importance of students knowing the stories of the administrative team. Each member of the team was to submit their high school graduation picture to be embedded in a PowerPoint presentation. During the assembly, each person would tell his or her story about where they were born, raised, schools attended, year of graduation, and finally, what their specific job was in our school.

On the day of the assembly, 700 students with their teachers filed into the auditorium while the music and lyrics of the song, "To Be Young, Gifted, and Black," by Nina Simone, sweetly reverberated from wall to wall.

To Be Young, Gifted, and Black

To be young, gifted, and Black
Oh, what a lovely precious dream
To be young, gifted, and Black
Open your heart to what I mean
In the whole world, you know
There are billion boys and girls
Who are young, gifted, and Black
And that's a fact!
Young, gifted, and Black
We must begin to tell our young
There's a world waiting for you
This is a quest that's just begun
When you feel really low
Yeah, there's a great truth you should know
When you're young, gifted, and Black
Your soul's intact
Young, gifted, and Black
How I long to know the truth
There are times when I look back
And I am haunted by my youth
Oh, but my joy of today
Is that we can all be proud to say
To be young, gifted, and Black
Is where it's at.

The assembly began with the recitation of the school's creed and singing of the "Yes, I Can" song.

We are beautiful
We are strong
We are respectful
We get along!
We are big dreamers
We will be

Everything we dream,
Just wait and see.
Teachers, lawyers, and
Dancers, Dear!
Vocalists and
Yes! Engineers!
I can be whatever I dream!
Yes, I can!
Yes, I can!

Afterward, one by one, each member of the administrative team introduced themselves. I spoke last, explaining to the student body that the members of the administrative team were once children, too, that we graduated from high school, and now we are their leadership. I praised them for their beauty and intelligence, encouraging them to succeed and achieve. The students were extremely well behaved. As we closed the assembly and students began to file out of the auditorium, "To Be Young, Gifted, and Black" blared from the speakers leaving all of us with a mystical sense of peace and pride.

∼

REFLECTION: We share the same world, breathe the same air, drink the same water, and eat the same produce from the earth, yet we are of different hues, language, and culture.

∼

REFLECTION QUESTION: In what ways can the history of the student population be taught, celebrated, and integrated into everyday learning?

Reality 6 – My Administrative Assistant Saved My Life

*a*s principal, I had a multitude of responsibilities that consumed each minute of the day. Being accountable to the hierarchy consisting of the school's authorizer, the management company, the superintendent, the director of curriculum, instruction, and assessment, then accountable to 700 students, 500 parents, and eighty staff members resulted in extremely busy days. The reality is that everyone relies on the principal in some fashion. I actually coined the phrase, "Everyone takes a bite out of the principal." But I am a small woman, five feet three inches whose weight is 126 pounds. I cannot take too much biting for fear of what would be left of me.

I appreciate that the management company's practice was to provide an administrative assistant. My load of responsibilities would have been unbearable without my administrative assistant's loyalty and support.

Resolution 6

As much as possible each morning, my administrative assistant, Mrs. Burrough, briefed me on my daily schedule, district meetings, conferences with teachers, issues, and phone calls that I needed to return. Initial phone calls to me were transferred to Mrs. Burrough. In addition, she devised a system to address the needs of parents. The plan consisted of completing a form with the parent's name, phone number, and issue they wanted me to address; the first phase.

In the second phase, Mrs. Burrough forwarded the request to the person who could address it. For example, if there was a discipline concern, the form was referred to the dean of students to address it effectively and in a timely manner. If the concern was a grading issue, it would be directed to the teacher. This system was a buffer as well as a means to address parental concerns with efficiency. As usual, some parental concerns had to be addressed immediately, and my administrative assistant ensured that the meeting occurred quickly with respect for the parent's time. However, in some instances, office personnel would inform me about an urgent parent's concern.

An example is when the front desk receptionist knocked on my office door, explaining that two parents were in the hallway crying. They were husband and wife who had just walked their third-grade daughter to her classroom. Tragically, their twenty-four-year-old son had been fatally shot. I invited both into my office.

"Please have a seat," as I pulled two chairs for them to sit in.

I was silent as they both wept, and tears began to well in my eyes. After a while, the husband spoke in a broken voice of deep pain.

"He was young. He was just getting his life together, and our daughter is having a very difficult time. It really hurts, Dr. McIntosh. It really hurts."

What do you say to a parent who has lost a child? "I am sorry for your loss," may be appropriate, but it doesn't, to any degree, meet the needs of grieving parents. The only thing I could do was to hold their hands, pray for their peace, and reassure them that I would check on their daughter consistently. They left my office visibly downtrodden but still offering their gratitude.

Appreciatively, my administrative assistant, and I built a positive relationship. She checked to see if I ate lunch, informed the chef to prepare it, cared for my well-being, and was committed to the efficiency, climate, and culture of the principal's office. She became one of my best friends in school and out.

∾

REFLECTION: Interdependency is the way of the world. Although we may not experience the farmer's toil, the harvester's sweat, and truck driver's weariness when transporting fruits and vegetables to grocery stores, we need them. Simply stated, our lives depend on them.

∽

REFLECTION QUESTION: How can the reality of interdependency be an ongoing awareness in the school community and practiced in the classroom?

Reality 7 – New Teacher Orientation

*N*ew teachers are hired each school year. How do we orientate them to the school's vision, mission, and school operations? One of the paraprofessionals, Ms. Robinson, was the eyes and ears throughout the school. She asked to meet with me and explained that she would like to take a needs assessment of all teachers—new and experienced ones. She completed the needs assessment, which was the catalyst for actions to acclimate new teachers to the school.

Resolution 7

With the assistance and collaboration of the administrative team, a new teacher binder consisting of approximately fifty pages was created. Content included the vision and mission statements, the names and duties of all office personnel, the grading system, the lesson plan format, the faculty meeting times and places, referral forms, incident report forms, grade-level teams, lead teachers' names, and the faculty directory. In addition, a new teacher orientation was instituted at the beginning of the new school year. All team members introduced themselves. Afterward, a PowerPoint presentation provided pertinent information designed specifically to support a new teacher in navigating the school environment. Time was provided for questions and answers, while refreshments were served. Finally, new teachers were given a tour of the building and shown their classrooms. To provide further support, lead teachers were introduced, and mentors were assigned to beginning teachers.

. . .

OUTLINE OF NEW Teacher Orientation

The purpose of the first day of orientation is to acquaint new teachers with the school environment, which includes familiarity with the physical environment, knowledge of the school schedule, requisition procedures and policies, and teachers' organization to implement the curriculum.

A. Familiarity with the Physical Environment

1. New teachers will meet the principal and the K-5 Administrative Staff. Each will state his/her responsibility.
2. The mission statement will be reviewed.
3. The parent/student handbook will be briefly reviewed.
4. The principal will conduct a tour of the school.
5. The principal will issue keys to classrooms.

B. Knowledge of the Schedule

1. New teachers will receive a schedule.
2. The assistant principal will review the schedule.

C. Requisition Procedures and Policy

1. New teachers will receive the folder of requisition procedures and policies.
2. The office manager will briefly review the contents in the folder.
3. The office manager will introduce each office personnel.
4. The office manager and records coordinator will teach new teachers the procedures regarding the grade book and attendance book.
5. New teachers will receive emergency procedures (fire, tornado, lock-in).

D. Organization of Teachers and Implementation of Curriculum

1. New teachers will receive the pacing guides and lesson plan format, which will be reviewed by the curriculum coordinator.
2. The roles of the lead teacher, grade-level facilitator, and learner-centered instructional team will be reviewed.
3. New teachers will meet the lead teacher.

E. Escort to Classrooms

The principal will escort, as much as possible, the new teachers to the perspective classrooms. Also, inform them of where to get vouchers for supplies.

∼

REFLECTION: Humans need support through systems. Teachers need support through structured lines of communication, information, and methods that promote professional growth. Without a supportive, intentional system, not only a new teacher but a veteran teacher will suffer emotionally.

∼

REFLECTION QUESTION: Why do teachers who begin the profession with fire find themselves in a place where the fire is dwindling or has burned out?

Reality 8 – Calming the Storm of Overlapping Responsibilities

I was a new principal entering a school that had two principals before me. I specifically asked for an assistant principal because the student population was 700. Consequently, my request was approved, and so was my choice of who the assistant principal should be. As we approached the third week of school of our first year, the assistant principal, Dr. Godine, met with me. She voiced a concern. She felt as if she was walking on eggshells. Unsure about her job responsibilities concerning the curriculum specialist who had served the school for several years, their relationship was tense. I listened intently.

∼

Resolution 8

I SET up a meeting with the assistant principal and the curriculum specialist. Prior to that, I made three copies of their job responsibilities, one set for each of us. Serving as the mediator, I asked that we review, discuss, and decide on each job's responsibility. We read each line carefully for clarification. There were approximately four areas where their job responsibilities overlapped. Of these overlapping responsibilities, both discussed and agreed which ones would be shared and which ones would be designated as an individual responsibility. I noted their changes. After the meeting, I submitted these modifications to the management company. Needless to say, there were no more eggshells, and both worked tirelessly and smoothly together.

~

REFLECTION: Listening with heart and ears leads to understanding, empathy, and resolution.

~

REFLECTION QUESTION: Do you recall a time when disputes arose between faculty members, or between you and a teacher or parent? How was it resolved?

Reality 9 – Curtailing Early Student Pickup

*S*chool dismisses at 3:30 p.m. Parents begin to flood the office lobby as early as 2:30 p.m. to pick up their children. However, the Parents' Handbook explicitly states that early dismissal is only permissible if there is an emergency, which is defined as a doctor's appointment, illness, or a family emergency. When a parent arrives, and the emergency complies with the Parents' Handbook, the parent signs in, an office receptionist calls the teacher announcing that a parent is on the way to the classroom. The teacher provides a sign-out sheet for the parent as documentation that the student was safely released.

Resolution 9

Initially, I met with the office team and discussed the policy of early pickup. "You are the first line of reinforcement," I explained. "This means that you are to politely remind the parent of the policy and ask if it's an emergency. A laminated copy is positioned on the counter for the parent to see. If the parent answers 'no,' invite them to wait until dismissal time or come back. Always thank them. If you are unsuccessful, then the parent is to see me."

As the second line of reinforcement, my encounter with a parent usually followed the same process. "Hi, how are you? I am Dr. McIntosh, the principal. What is your name?" I offer a handshake. "You were made aware of the policy by the office secretary. Can you please explain why you have come to pick up your child early?" Responses ranged from avoiding the traffic to getting hair done. I continued with my explanation. "When you enrolled your child at the school, you also agreed to abide by the arrival and dismissal time. Teaching and learning are still in process. When the phone call is made to the teacher, she instructs the student to prepare to leave, gathers the sign-out clipboard, and then waits until you sign it. Instruction stops. It's unfair for the other twenty-four students. It's your child's time to be educated. We would like to give them the best chance." If the parent persists, I state that "I will approve this time, but I will not be able to do it again." The majority of the time, this was effective. Other times, the parent had to wait to speak to me until there was only twenty minutes left until dismissal. I reminded them of this, and some agreed to wait. But, I remember one day, the first line of reinforcement wasn't so effective. I must have seen about nine parents, one right after the other, and I gave the same presentation. I was getting exhausted, frustrated, and a bit disappointed. I was tempted to say, "Just take your child and go." I am glad I yielded not to temptation.

~

REFLECTION: WHEN WE REACH OUR WITS' end, acknowledge it. Stop. Take a deep breath. Step back. Go home if you can.

~

REFLECTION QUESTION: What are you most proud of when interacting with parents?

REALITY 10 – WHY IS THIS STUDENT LATE?

The school policy emphasizes the importance of punctuality and outlines consequences for tardiness, including parental notices, a meeting with the principal, and sometimes a conference with the board of directors. It is a tedious process, but tardiness still existed. How can we decrease the tardy numbers?

RESOLUTION 10

Because the modular, a ten classroom building for kindergarten and first graders, was separated from the main building, two staff members were posted in the modular to write tardy passes. One was also stationed in the main building at the main entrance. Eventually, the policy of having two at the modular was changed because doors were locked at 8:15 a.m. So everyone had to enter the main building for tardy passes. An additional person was assigned to assist. Between 8:15 and 8:30 a.m., a line of approximately twenty students needed tardy passes. Those kindergartners and first graders had to be escorted to the modular, which I did many times. Some days the line was shorter, but tardiness was not eradicated.

One chilly, rainy day, a young African American man with two female students who looked to be in the second and third grade entered the building at 9 a.m., an hour after school started. I was appalled. Didn't he know that education is important and that he must have the girls on time to support them in achieving a quality life? As the students received their tardy passes, I invited the young man into my office and asked why the students were so late. I was prepared to give a lengthy discourse on the importance of punctuality. He explained that the girls were his nieces, his sister's car had broken down, that she had no money to get it fixed yet, so he walked them to school. I asked, "How far do you live from here?" He replied, "About one and a half miles." I paused; this is not the time to offer constructive criticism or to throw the handbook at him. I thought I had the means to get my car repaired, but some parents didn't. He had walked them to school on a chilly and rainy day. As humbly as possible, I said, "I am glad you made it." This situation taught me to refrain from labeling parents. Hearing their stories is more productive and provides a door to understanding the individuals that make up the school community.

∾

REFLECTION: Observing the physical attributes of a person is only a shallow glimpse into who they are, their experiences, and their stories.

∾

REFLECTION QUESTION: What are your memories of learning the stories of teachers, students, and parents?

*E*very principal has the responsibility to evaluate teachers. The district's process included two evaluations; one was announced, and the other unannounced. It also included an evaluation tool that consisted of a numerical performance rubric and a narrative section. For the announced observation, times were scheduled, and the teacher was notified. Before the actual lesson observation, a pre-conference was scheduled to discuss the lesson plan. Next, the lesson is observed, and finally, a post-conference is held with the teacher to discuss the rubric results and the narrative. A tremendous amount of time is required to complete evaluations and then submit to the management company by the deadline. My administrative assistant was responsible for all the scheduling. Because the staff numbered eighty, the assistant principal and I divided the evaluations between us.

Evaluations tend to make teachers nervous and sometimes filled with anxiety. For me, I wanted them to perceive evaluations as a tool for growth and, most importantly, that they were fair.

RESOLUTION 11

During the post-conference of the teacher evaluation process, I provided a copy of the completed tool for the teachers and myself. I met with each teacher individually and stated the score for each competency. I felt it was extremely important for me to invite the teacher's voice, so I asked if they agreed with the score and if they had any questions. If a teacher disagreed with a score, I welcomed their comments. When the statement was feasible, I willingly changed the score. Other times, I offered specific teaching practices and advice in areas where growth was needed. Overall, the assistant principal and I gained the trust of teachers and witnessed the implementation of practices and strategies that supported their professional development and increased student learning.

~

REFLECTION: In reality, the relationship between principals and teachers is a partnership of mutual respect.

~

REFLECTION QUESTION: Do you perceive your role as principal more as a leader who influences or a boss of compliance? Why?

Reality 12 – A Kindergarten Runner

he first day of school has always been very exciting. To see students arrive in new and fresh uniforms accompanied by their parents creates a busy, bustling, beautiful ambiance. On the first day of school, during my second year as a principal, I received a kindergarten teacher's phone call. "Hi, Dr. McIntosh, I have a runner. This is her first day in school and she keeps running after her mother." I replied, "I will be right there." Some kindergartners become so distressed when they realize their mothers are leaving them.

Resolution 12

I left my office and walked quickly to the modular. Upon entering the main hallway, I immediately saw a kindergarten little girl—brown skin, wearing a neatly pressed uniform and hair expertly pulled into a wavy ponytail. She was running toward her mother with tears streaming down her face. Her teacher looked on. I turned to my right and saw the mother, who also seemed as distressed as her daughter. Facing the mother, I reassured her that her baby would be fine and that I would take over from here. With hesitation, she slowly walked away. Now, I gave my full attention to the "itty bitty." That's my endearing term for little people. "Hi, sweetheart. You want to stay with your mother and I understand. Look at my watch." I held out my wrist and pointed to the number three.

"Your mother will be back at that time, and I know she is coming." I gently took her small hand and walked her to the classroom where other students are sitting on the carpet. I escorted her there as she gripped my hand tightly. I detected this, so I sat down on the carpet cross-legged right behind her. The teacher attempted to soothe her by saying that another student in the class had the same name. She stopped crying, and I thought it was a good time to leave. But, as I scooted back, she scooted back also. Oh, I thought, that's a cute and smart way to stop me from leaving. Again, I scooted back. Again, she scooted back until her back came into contact with my crossed legs. Finally, I had to tell her the truth. "Sweetheart, I have to go because I have to take care of some principal things, but I will be back to see you." She looked at me and gave me permission. I left quietly. Now, I have gained a little itty bitty's trust, and each time she sees me, she is comforted.

∾

REFLECTION: Each of us has a need to be nurtured; simply, because we are all human beings.

∾

REFLECTION QUESTION: Thinking about yourself, in what areas do you need to be nurtured? In what ways do teachers, students, and parents need nurturing?

Reality 13 – Combing Hair?

For the majority of my life, I worked with children in the capacities of teacher, babysitter, group leader, and national youth director for a faith-based organization. Nurturing and caring for children must be in my DNA. So, when I encounter a child who is in need, I act. On the first day of my first year as principal, I noticed a little kindergarten girl whose hair needed some maintenance. It seemed as if it had not been brushed or combed for a couple of days. Her hair was pulled into three ponytails, but spots of hair stuck out from the sides. I thought she might feel better if her hair was neater. I erroneously thought this would be a quick fix, and I would return to my morning hall post in three minutes. I was wrong.

Resolution 13

In my office, I had a clean brush, comb, and rubber bands. I invited her to sit in one of the leather chairs in my office. My sincere intent was to tidy up her hair so that she would feel great in school. As I proceeded to remove the rubber bands, her hair sprang forth like a lion's mane, much to my surprise. It was so thick, and there was so much of it that her face seemed like a tiny moon with the entire black sky surrounding it. What have I gotten myself into? The speculated three minutes of preparation escalated to twenty minutes of trying to comb and brush her hair back into those three ponytails. I finally managed to get it under control. Needless to say, I did not get back to my morning post, and she was a few minutes late for her class. My advice to those principals who have a burning desire to tidy up hair, don't. Overall, it will always be a lasting memory. She is in middle school now and still remembers that I combed her hair.

~

REFLECTION: The well-being of students involves a committed community of adults that involves administrators, teachers, and parents.

~

REFLECTION QUESTION: In what ways can the adult community commit themselves to the well-being of students?

REALITY 14 – GOSSIP, TAKE IT TO THE SOURCE

*L*ife is a teacher. As a teenager, I remember my youngest sister Jackie, Nora and Virginia, our neighbors, and I were close friends. But, there would be times when friends disagreed. Nora came to me and talked about Virginia. Then Virginia would come and talk about Nora. I thought that if they gossiped about each other to me, then they would also gossip about me. My position as a teenager was to stay out of it. If my friends had a problem with each other, then the two should talk about it. As a principal, I discovered the same dynamic. Faculty members approached me periodically to report that their colleagues were saying things about them to other teachers. This creates a school climate of mistrust and gossip among the adults.

~

RESOLUTION 14

As a principal, I committed myself to the practice of refraining from mentioning anything negative to another faculty member. Also, I shared no information about what a teacher disclosed to me. I valued being an example of trust, peace, and professionalism. I planned a faculty meeting to address gossip and positive talk within the school community explicitly. I distributed handouts defining the following terms and characteristics of an effective school:

Gossip: chatty talk, a rumor or report of an intimate nature

Gossiper: a person who habitually reveals personal or sensational facts about others

Malicious: given to, marked by, or arising from malice

Malice: desire to cause pain, injury, or distress to another

AN EFFECTIVE SCHOOL ACCEPTS...

- Necessity of organization
- Authority
- Well-defined chain of command
- Basis of strong leadership as possessing humility and a willingness to serve

In the meeting, teachers were grouped by grade levels and instructed to take turns reading an article about gossip out loud in their small group. Afterward, individuals shared reading highlights to the entire faculty. I provided the following resolution; "Take it to the source." If you hear anything said about you, take time to find out what was said and who said it, and converse with your colleague with the intent to resolve it. If you choose not to take it to the source, then choose to let it go. "Take it to the source" became the catalyst for motivating teachers to speak honestly with one another or to simply let it go. Finally, we concluded with the expectations of Winans' teachers.

OUR WAPA (WINANS ACADEMY OF PERFORMING ARTS) RESPONSIBILITY:

- We do not involve ourselves in the malicious discussion of rumors or gossip.
- We constantly work to maintain high morale within our school community and destroy negative attitudes.
- We work to become more efficient by becoming more organized.
- We work to resolve all weaknesses and mistakes, no matter who is directly responsible or at fault.

- We direct questions to those responsible in accordance with the district's organizational structure.

It would be presumptuous of me to declare that gossip was annihilated. The reality is that it was significantly curtailed.

∽

REFLECTION: Negative comments are painful, and the body reacts as if it was physically assaulted.

∽

REFLECTIVE QUESTION: How might honesty be practiced resulting in peace and understanding rather than anger and hostility?

REALITY 15 – VALUING STUDENTS

$\mathcal{S}$tudents are people—smaller and younger human beings. Sometimes they are pleasant, sometimes defiant, and occasionally nerve-wrecking. Even with these descriptions, I believe each has value. One of my most trusted mentors, the late Reverend Albert B. Cleage, advised me to be a level above students. Similar to the words, "When they go low, we go high" from First Lady Michelle Obama. Frequently, students are addressed in demeaning ways because of the teacher's unconscious and conscious negativity and trauma experiences, such as abandonment, feeling unloved, hearing anger in parents' voices, being the object of profanity, and experiencing physical assault, and witnessing parents' use of drugs. This can result in labeling students, declaring their lack of potential, and expressing disdain through body language and tone of voice.

RESOLUTION 15

Everything is done for the benefit of the child. The cycle of life places a responsibility on adults. Although society falls short of this because some adults have not assumed this responsibility, the school community still must accept it. As a practice, I advocated that the tone of teachers' voices be pleasant and friendly. To avoid alienating students, teachers were prohibited from punishing students by making them stand outside the classroom or in a corner. Morning classroom meetings were instituted during the first ten minutes of class for community building in which students shared aspects of their lives to create a sense of belonging where all are viewed as friends. The staff was trained in restorative practices, and a teacher committee instituted the Positive Behavior Intervention System to build knowledge and skills in listening and resolving conflicts.

When done consistently, morning classroom meetings help students develop positive relationships and a sense of belonging. I explained to the staff, that students would be self-governing within three months. My third-grade teacher exclaimed one day, "Dr. McIntosh, I didn't believe it when you said it, but the students in my classroom manage their behaviors. Thank you."

∾

REFLECTION: Sharing a vision where others accept that vision makes it possible to create a transformative school community.

∾

REFLECTION QUESTION: What are your practices for sharing a vision so that staff and parents are participants in transforming the school community?

Reality 16 – Who Is the Staff?

*I*nterviews provide only minutes of a glimpse into someone else's life. Although necessary and practical for hiring, knowing more about each staff person is a process. This knowledge for a principal is invaluable. As a new principal, I honestly did not have a plan to learn more about teachers' stories, backgrounds, challenges, and what was important to them outside of the initial introduction in the first faculty meeting. However, as I grew into my position, I've learned that certain activities reveal teachers' stories.

Resolution 16

1. Scheduled meetings that are held consistently. For example, grade-level team meetings and teacher leadership meetings are viable situations for formal and informal human interactions; a setting where individuals feel free to disclose more of their personal selves.
2. Pre- and post-conference evaluation sessions that allowed teachers' voices and input create a teacher-friendly environment where they find it comfortable to talk about children, after-work challenges, and aspirations.
3. Monthly scheduled Muffins with McIntosh. Muffins, donuts, hot chocolate, tea, coffee, and yogurt were available in my office for the entire staff. This provided an informal platform for teachers to share anything they wanted to share.

Some things I learned about my teachers is that among them are: a judge of musical concerts, a jazz trumpet player, a dancer, an actress, a cancer patient who asked to continue working, detailed organizers, biracial marriages, a creative doll maker, passion for teaching technology, former school administrator, infidelity in a marriage, parent challenges raising teenagers, pregnancies, weddings, engagements, vast knowledge of teaching, a singer with a renowned vocal group, ideas and challenges in education, a head of a church ministry, and marathon runners and joggers.

When a teacher shared their upcoming performances, whether a jazz concert, dance, or acting, I attended when my schedule allowed. Teachers are whole human beings, and their satisfaction with life affects their teaching competence and success.

∾

REFLECTION: Knowing oneself is the catalyst for self-transformation. Knowing others is the catalyst for transforming the school community.

∾

REFLECTION QUESTION: What is your vision of an ideal school?

Reality 17 – Faculty Meetings

*W*eekly faculty meetings are required in most schools. The purpose is to create a teacher community that is informed and in continual growth. Preparing agendas for each meeting requires reflection, insight, vision, and a grasp of the current climate. I reflected on the staff's social and professional status, decided about organizational information, and devised an agenda for each faculty meeting.

Resolution 17

Faculty Meeting Agenda

Purpose: Heart-to-Heart Session—In building a professional learning committee, we must be committed to honesty as a way to create positive, supportive relationships.

Principal's Opening Statement: I have seen orderly lines, children being called "Sweetie," consistent community-building sessions, beautifully decorated halls in the mods, and teachers not missing a teachable moment. I have seen a class where students sat and talked to each other at the cafeteria table rather than turning around and talking to the students at different tables, the warm relationships between teachers and students, introductions to lesson plans on photosynthesis using a real plant and a colorful diagram on the board, teachers creating exciting and original learning activities, and children stretched out on the floor reading and listening to their teachers. I have seen effective questioning skills and scaffolding, a welcome carpet, pictures of children on the walls, students choosing their own classroom jobs, and teachers finding funding resources. I have seen many, many wonderful things!

> "Still the question recurs, "Can we do better?" The dogmas of the quiet past are inadequate to the stormy present. The occasion is piled high with difficulty, and we must rise with the occasion. As our case is new, so we must think anew, and act anew." — **Abraham Lincoln**

A. Our Changes

1. Cafeteria–Creating an orderly and safe environment, including the cafeteria.
2. Removal of portable refrigerators from classrooms to provide a safe and proper environment.
3. To decrease the number of worksheet copies, grade-level teams must engage in dialogue and critically analyze instructional strategies.
4. Students changing uniforms in the gym. This location is the best place and helps to prevent students from wearing gym uniforms under school uniforms.
5. Teachers to refrain from yelling at students.

B. Our Challenge–Can we become a professional learning community where honesty prevails? Can we communicate with our peers concerning relationship issues and academic issues? Can we honestly communicate to maintain healthy relationships?

C. Can we actually become an effective group? "I will pay more for the ability to deal with people than for any other ability under the sun."– John D. Rockefeller

D. Interpersonal Patterns Activity

> "I never let the sun set on a disagreement with anybody who means a lot to me." –**Thomas Watson St.**, Founder, IBM

E. Teacher Triads: Read Comparison of Effective and Ineffective Groups (The Nature and Significance of Groups in Organizations).

Effective Groups	Ineffective Groups
Encourage discussion on points on which they disagree and use healthy conflict to introduce creativity and change in ideas before reaching a consensus. They see conflict in a positive light. Such a group is characterized by:	Establish an agreed viewpoint quickly and defend it against any new or original idea. Task completion can thus be achieved quickly, although this often means that the symptom has been treated rather than the underlying cause. Such groups are characterized by:
Open discussion—members participate and make contributions to the group, with the discussions being reasonable, and members being prepared to listen to and learn from other group members.	a lack of agreed objectives and an atmosphere full of tensions—these tensions are sometimes held in check, but on occasions flare into destructive conflict, and there are clashes of personality, with members not really listening to what others are saying;
Reaching a decision by a process of convincing members by logical argument, rather than crude voting which can leave a size-able minority disgruntled.	decision making through voting, but with little effort to win round the minority who vote against the idea; avoidance of assessing and discussing its progress and performance.
Using situational leadership—different people may lead the group under various circumstances, with different styles of leadership appropriate to the circumstances;	
Pursuing common goals, whoever is leading it;	
Assessing its own progress to achieving its goals and making the necessary changes to improve its performance.	

Overview of School Culture
Correlates of Effective Schools

Correlates Addressed in this Report:

Clear School Mission–In an effective school, there is a clearly articulated school **mission** through which the staff shares an understanding of and **commitment** to **instructional goals, priorities, assessment procedures,** and **accountability.**

High Expectations for Success–In an effective school, there is a climate of expectation that the staff believes and demonstrates that all students can attain **mastery** of the essential content and school skills. The staff also believes that they can help all students **achieve** that **mastery.**

~

Principal Observations
(read to staff)

Teachers have common grade-level planning time, which is spent on lesson planning for the most part. However, there are often behaviors that inhibit shared commitment to instructional goals, priorities, assessment procedures, and accountability. These behaviors include sharing negative comments about other teachers and administration. For example, Mrs. Matthew was encountered by a first-grade teacher letting her know that the first-grade team did not like Reading Mastery; thus, implying that she should not support it either. The grade-level team meetings sometimes become avenues for venting against administrative changes or disagreements.

For a first-year teacher, this is detrimental. Outside of grade-level meetings, teachers have had friend relationships for several years. This is admirable except when it stops them from having critical dialogue about their teaching. They tend to protect more rather than correct each other about student learning. A critical observation by administration is taken personally and then shared with other teachers. The focus does not seem to be solely for the benefit of the child. When this happens, teachers fail to feel personally accountable for student success.

High expectations for success are watered down by teacher perception of students and parents. Although there has been some change, there is too much blame being placed on the student rather than taking a critical view of how a subject is being taught. There is also an attitude of "we teach them the best we can, but students are not capable of learning." Therefore, mastery is not the objective. What seems to be most important to teachers is that they teach the way they want without instructional advice and input. Also, there is a lack of cultural and personal knowledge of students and parents.

This overview is not done to be critical for critical sake, but to point to cultural behaviors that need to be transformed to build a greater school. Staff must exhibit personal behaviors that create a positive and supportive adult climate and professional behaviors that support student learning. This is critical for the growth or our school.

~

Staff Covenant

HAVING RECEIVED our mission to be an advocate for children through the ministry of teaching, I pledge to faithfully participate in the Winans Academy of Performing Arts by my effective instruction, my presence, my gifts, and my service.

1. I will protect the unity of my school by:

- acting in love toward all in the WAPA Family
- refusing to gossip
- supporting goals and directions

2. I will share the responsibility of my school by:

- working for its growth
- inviting parents, community members, and university partners to visit and participate
- warmly welcoming those who visit

3. I will serve the ministry of my school by:

- using my gifts and talents
- preparing myself through professional development, sharing ideas with peers, and collaborating with school administrators
- developing a caring heart

4. I will support the mission of my school by:

- good attendance and punctuality
- being an example of excellence
- always having high expectations

Our mission is to prepare students for academic and performing arts excellence and responsible citizenship.

How Will We Accomplish Our Mission?

We will accomplish our mission by a commitment to five basic purposes: to nurture, to teach, to collaborate, to build community, and to problem-solve.

To nurture the whole child, academically, socially, physically, and spiritually by using best practices, an encouraging environment, nutritious food and exercise, and times of reflection through art, writing, and quiet moments

To teach for success by using the latest research-based strategies and providing hands-on and minds-on activities based on inquiry and reteaching whenever needed and based on Michigan Standards and the curriculum of Saginaw Valley State University

To collaborate effectively with teachers, parents, and administration with the interest of the child being central, by use of no-fault, consensus, and collaboration or no paralysis guidelines

To build community in classrooms and the larger school by frequent community-building activities and positive language and behavior that reflect love and kinship

To problem-solve by seeking answers that provide the best environment for students to be adequately prepared to be successful in school and life with civic responsibility.

> "The only thing that endures over time is the law of the farm: I must prepare the ground, put in the seed, cultivate it, water it, then gradually nurture growth and development to full maturity… there is no quick fix."–**Stephen Covey**

We must cultivate, water, and nurture the growth of our relationships to full maturity. This gives us the power to educate our children and build a school of excellence.

～

REFLECTION: When a group of adults is joined body, mind, and spirit to a common purpose larger than themselves, unseen power activates and is reflected in productive actions for the benefit of the child.

～

REFLECTION QUESTION: How do you identify your own behaviors that are productive or destructive in building a harmonious, yet purpose-driven, adult group?

REALITY 18 – BLACK HISTORY MONTH

*R*esearch shows that students' feelings of worthiness and belonging are nurtured by faculty members who look like them. The majority of inner-city schools have student populations that are predominantly African American. Although Black History is only celebrated in February, it is critical that students learn about the past and present contributions of African Americans to America's intellectual and economic progress.

The contributions of African Americans to the building of America are underrepresented in textbooks. Foremost, Africans enslaved in America were skilled blacksmiths, goldsmiths, farmers, architectures, teachers, kings, queens, trained military, and scientists. The institution of slavery brutally forced them to use these skills to create wealth for slave owners. In essence, America was built on skilled slave labor, creating corporate and generational wealth for White people. But, textbooks fail to embrace this historical truth that enslaved Africans played a major role in building America.

I pondered over how a connection could be made between the past and present, reflecting on African Americans' intelligence, skills, and resilience to create a sense of pride among my students.

Ideas for Black History Month were first discussed with the administrative team. Then the purpose was discussed with performing arts and academic teachers who offered their creative ideas. The kickoff of this month began with an assembly.

RESOLUTION 18

Black History Assembly Program

Prelude: Recorded music/CD of To Be *Young, Gifted, and Black*

Introduction of Why We Celebrate

Recognition of Black history originated in 1926 by historian Carter G. Woodson as "Negro History Week." It was later celebrated as Black History Month. Woodson chose the second week of February because it marked two Americans' birthdays who greatly influenced African Americans' lives and social conditions: former President Abraham Lincoln and abolitionist and former slave Frederick Douglass.

Until the study of Black history, Blacks were absent from history books. Carter G. Woodson founded the Association for the Study of African American Life and History in 1915 and was one of the first scholars to study the African diaspora's history, including African American history. A year later, he founded the widely respected *Journal of Negro History*. "Negro History Week" was intended to bring national attention to Black people's contributions throughout history.

We celebrate all the contributions of Africans and African Americans. We celebrate that many survived slavery and that they gave us life. We celebrate art, music, dance, inventions, science, technology, and mathematics that African Americans brought to the world. We celebrate the past, the present, and the future.

The Past
(read by administrative team member)
Africa my Africa
Africa my mother land
land of milk and honey
land of natural beauty

Africa land where I live

Africa my Africa
A land of great rulers
Africa my Africa
land of nature
A land where nature lives

Africa my Africa
A land blessed by God himself
On the day of creation
God threw diamonds like stone
gold like rain
He dropped crude oil like rain

Africa my Africa
land of milk and honey.

AFRICAN DANCE (DANCE Club)

Slavery–Dreams Are Not Enough
(read by administrative team member)
In the beginning
children ran free
playing games
dancing with flowers
looking up at the clouds
and making dreams.

It is a land
not so very far away
a neighborhood
like yours
where the children
look just
like you and me.

59

They smile
and make funny faces
to each other
happy
feeling safe
and loved.

The people
are kind
but the village
is sad
caught up
in an unfair world
full of greed
and war.

A world
where evil
still lives
and men
make plans
to hurt
the people
and the village.

And the worst
of these plans
is slavery
where men
women
and even children
are owned
like animals
and have no rights
of their own.

And so the slave traders
came capturing
the peoples
of the village
hurting the men
stealing mothers
and children
taking their lives
and chaining them
into slavery.

They are sent
to camps and factories
cities and countries
all over the world
children no longer
with their mothers
forced to work
and hunger
they no longer
run free.

The children are sad
and cry out—alone
as slavers steal lives
and destroy villages
but they cannot
steal dreams
and in their dreams
the children
always run free.

But dreams
are not enough
for children
little or big.

Through teary eyes
a child remembers
what it was like
to run free
a shackled hand
moves out
the darkness
reaching for freedom
voices echo
END SLAVERY NOW!

Summary about Slavery: (teachers)

Song: "Follow the Drinking Gourd" (performed by the fifth-grade choir)

Quilt Presentation: (presented by fourth grade)

Slide Presentation: African American Contributions to Civilization and America (narrated by computer teacher and fifth-grade students)

Song: "I'm Gonna Sing" (spiritual medley performed by first-grade students)

Grandparents' Stories:

- Mrs. Carla Fluker, grandmother of Leilani Maxey, sharing a story about why knowing your ancestry is important
- Mr. Joe Golson, grandfather of Eric Golson, sharing a story about his service in the Vietnam War
- Ms. Lucille Smith, grandmother of Bryce Moore, sharing a story about the Ruby Bridges Story

"Still I Rise" by Mayo Angelou
(excerpts read by administrative team member)

You may write me down in history
With your bitter, twisted lies,

You may trod me in the very dirt
But still, like dust, I'll rise.

Does my sassiness upset you?
Why are you beset with gloom?
'Cause I walk like I've got oil wells
Pumping in my living room.

Just like moons and like suns,
With the certainty of tides,
Just like hopes springing high,
Still I'll rise.

Did you want to see me broken?
Bowed head and lowered eyes?
Shoulders falling down like teardrops,
Weakened by my soulful cries.

Does my haughtiness offed you?
Don't you take it awful hard
Cause I laugh like I've got gold mines
Diggin in my own backyard.

You may shoot me with your words,
You may cut me with your eyes,
You may kill me with your hatefulness,
But still, like air, I'll rise.

Out of the huts of history's shame
I rise
Up from a past that's rooted in pain
I rise
I'm a black ocean, leaping and wide,
Welling and swelling I bear in the tide.

Leaving behind nights of terror and fear

I rise
Into a daybreak that's wondrously clear
I rise
Bringing the gifts that my ancestors gave,
I am the dream and the hope of the slave.
I rise
I rise
I rise.

Song: "When the Saints Go Marching In" (performed by fourth-grade class)

The Present and the Future
(read by administrative team member)

The future is you. Children of ebony hue!

You built the pyramids and the sphinx. You gave the world math and made them think. You were very smart and very keen. You were royalty, kings, and queens. There is nothing you cannot do.

The future is you. Children of ebony hue!

Plan your lives in a smart way. Make your tomorrows better than today. Greatness runs within your heart. Now, step up and do your part! There is nothing you cannot DO.

The future is You! Children of ebony hue!

Now stand up tall and straight. Protect your future like an iron gate. Let your eyes look up to the sky and welcome all of those who did die so you can have a better life, free of poverty, and free of strife. There is nothing you cannot DO!

The future is You! Children of ebony hue!

Children Repeat:

There is nothing we cannot do. We are the children of ebony hue. The future belongs to me and YOU.

Closing: Black Man by Stevie Wonder (played as students exit)

Black History Month Public Announcements

During Black History Month, I created morning announcements to highlight the inventions of African Americans.

Good Morning Family,

This is Dr. McIntosh reporting from radio station WAPA 100, to give you some Black History highlights! Have you ever thought about who makes things?

Boys and girls, when I got up this morning, I looked at my watch so that I would know what time it was. Benjamin Banneker, a Black man, invented the first watch.

After taking my shower and putting on my clothes, I went downstairs and turned off the security alarm on my house. A security alarm makes a loud noise for me and also sends a message to the alarm company that someone may be breaking into the house. Marie Brown, a Black woman, invented the video home security system.

I sat down in a chair to eat my breakfast. Nathaniel Alexander, a Black man, invented the folding chair like the ones in the vocal room and the orchestra room.

I turned on the television to listen to the news. Otis Boykin, a Black man, invented an improved electrical resistor used in television sets.

Benjamin Banneker, Marie Brown, Nathaniel Alexander, and Otis Boykin—WOW! They used their brains to create, to invent things we use every day. Black people helped build the world. You, too, have the brains to create. You belong to a great people, a strong people, a beautiful people.

This is Dr. McIntosh. Make it a great day or not. The choice is yours!

∼

REFLECTION: Each ethnic student must be grounded in the collective history of their culture to instill a sense of belonging, and at the same time, examine its glories and mistakes.

∼

REFLECTION QUESTION: In what ways has an environment been established in which students know their history?

*principal can be more effective in sharing the vision and collaborating with a team. With a focus on academic operations and student support, the administrative team is critical. My team initially consisted of the assistant principal, curriculum director, dean of students, and special education coordinator. Later, the reading specialist and teacher coach were added. Each was required to submit a report and present it in the meeting. Weekly meetings served dual purposes: One was to create consistency in building a team; the other was to instill a sense of importance. I devised an agenda for each meeting.

RESOLUTION 19

K–5 ADMINISTRATIVE MEETING

A. Welcome

An effective school accepts:

- Necessity of organization
- Authority
- Well-defined chain of command
- Basis of strong leadership is humility and a willingness to serve

Copies of the district's organizational structure distributed for discussion.

Our responsibility:

- We do not involve ourselves in the malicious discussion of rumors or gossip.
- We constantly work to maintain high morale within our school community and destroy negative attitudes.
- We work to become more efficient by becoming more organized.
- We work to resolve all weaknesses and mistakes, no matter who is directly responsible or at fault.

B. Direction and focus of the meeting: Do everything possible to achieve academic and performing arts excellence and responsible citizenship. (Redirect conversation/discussion so that we can stay on point.)

C. Minutes

D. Old and New Business

1. K–5 administrative staff to present ourselves as being on the same page.
2. Social Studies Alive! Teacher and student materials ordered.
3. Social Studies Textbooks
4. Washington Trip
5. Lansing Trip Chaperones
6. City Hall Trip
7. Fire Drills Scheduled
8. Tornado Drill
9. Lock Down Drill
10. Push for the End of the School Year: Assist teachers to do their best.
11. The month of May begins the planning phase for the new school year.
12. Initiatives:

Initiative 1 – Tutoring for students testing non-proficient and partially proficient in reading will be done. The program used for intervention will be Corrective Reading.

Initiative 2 – Departmentalize the new school year for third, fourth, and fifth grades. Grade level teams will discuss who will teach English Language Arts, social studies, science, and mathematics.

Initiative 3 – A four week Michigan Educational Assessment Program (MEAP) Camp will be held for students who tested partially proficient in reading.

Initiative 4 – A four-week summer school program will be held for students testing non-proficient in reading.

Initiative 5 – The performing arts team will develop a curriculum for performing arts.

E. Reports

1. Curriculum Coordinator
2. Dean of Students
3. Special Education Coordinator
4. Assistant Principal

F. Closing

∽

REFLECTION: Meeting consistently is the key to maintaining discussion, sustaining collaboration, continuing cooperation, motivating accountability, and welcoming evaluation.

∽

REFLECTION QUESTION: In ordinary life, and specifically in the life of principals, what hinders or contributes to consistency?

REALITY 20 – TEACHER LEADERSHIP TEAM

*T*he education, experience, and expertise of teachers are invaluable. Oftentimes, teachers have very little time to collaborate and plan together because of the school schedule. In urban schools, this is a real challenge; however, it was important for me that teachers viewed themselves as leaders and vision keepers because they influenced other teachers.

~

RESOLUTION 20

For teachers to collaborate and have a voice, I instituted a Teacher Leadership Team consisting of lead teachers and grade-level facilitators. Lead teachers facilitated and chaired grade-band meetings. For example, four lead teachers were representing the following grade bands: (1) kindergarten-first; (2) second-third; (3) fourth-fifth; and (4) performing arts. Also, there were five grade-level facilitators responsible for meeting with their specific grade-level teachers. During my tenure, each grade level consisted of five classrooms. Because two performing arts classes were scheduled each day, teachers received two preparation periods. Grade-level meetings were held once a week and grade-band meetings because of common preparation periods. The Teacher Leadership Team meeting was held once a month for one hour after school. An agenda was prepared for each meeting.

Teacher Leadership Team (TLT) Meeting

I. Welcome

Scenario: A reporter has boarded the Winans Educational Ship. He is doing a special report on education and highlighting our accomplishments. However, the ship will leave in the next two and a half minutes. He must hear from each of you about your grade-level accomplishments. You have twenty-five seconds each to tell him. Think about it for a few seconds. You will be timed.

What we accomplish as a team is powerful!

II. What steps can we take together to make this an even better school?

III. We prepare students for academic and performing arts excellence and responsible citizenship.

Vision: Raising the Bar
Reading

- 80% of a student's score proficient in reading as measured by the Michigan Educational Assessment Progress (MEAP).
- Research-based intervention to improve reading skills (corrective reading)
- "High readers" receive an organized and developed enrichment program
- Students read two or more grade levels above

Mathematics

- 85% of students score proficient in math as measured by the MEAP
- Use of diagnostics, math mastery assessments to guide instruction
- "High math students" receive an organized and developed an accelerated program
- Students perform math operations two or more grade levels above

Science

- 80% of students score proficient in science as measured by the MEAP

Writing

- 80% of students score proficient in writing as measured by the MEAP

IV. Sharing Information

- Assistant principal
- Curriculum director
- Special education coordinator
- Teacher coach
- Lead teachers
- Grade-level facilitators

V. Closing (repeated in unison)

We are the TLT
One leadership team
Connected by passion
And sharing one dream.

Call us the TLT
The great ship on sea
Where student achievement
Is top priority.
Give us your child and we will give you a scholar.

~

REFLECTION: Self-Determination Theory posits that all human beings have three psychological needs: (1) to be competent, (2) to be autonomous, and (3) to relate.

~

REFLECTION QUESTION: From the perspective of the principal, another professional, or parent, are the needs to be competent, to be autonomous, and to relate to others being met?

REALITY 21 – POSITIVE ENVIRONMENT FOR TEACHERS

*R*esearch indicates that the teacher is the most important person that influences student success. Encouraging teachers, revisiting the vision, and creating a collaborative climate are nurturing. Newsletters specifically for teachers, public announcements showing appreciation, and developing a staff oath based on the mission and vision are specific actions I implemented as principal.

❧

RESOLUTION 21

McIntosh Tidbits
Excerpt — Newsletter for Teachers

We have finished another fabulous school year, and it happened because of YOU. I am so proud to be working with such great people. In closing out this year, I wanted all to know the greatness of our fellow team players. We work in different areas, and because we do, we don't see all that others do! This is an attempt for us to see some of each other's greatness! Thank you!

Kindergarten

Brophy: Positive Behavior Intervention System (PBIS) Committee, Moving Up Day Committee, support for new teachers, awesome attendance of parents for class awards, and performance.

Grays: Lead teacher; chair of Moving Up Day Committee, great attendance of parents for class awards

Jiang: Writing workshops for parents, morning tutoring, Buddies for Reading

Morris: Recruiter for new kindergartners, great attendance of parents for class awards and performance

Ponder: Best class in the hallway and the birth of new baby, Little Riyan.

First Grade

Giessl: Grade-level facilitator, assisted cheerleaders, magnificent instructional units

Herbert: Picked up the reins later in the school year and maintained classroom

Jones: Picked up the reins later in the school year and maintained the classroom

McCargo: Picked up the reins later in the school year and maintained the classroom

Javadi: Phenomenal growth as a first-year teacher, willing to try new strategies

Second Grade

Lary: Grade-level facilitator, mentor, awesome teacher

Knaebel: Organized in-house field trip, ordered kits for second grade, prepared packet of what to do over the summer for parents

Randall: Trained for Teachscape, taught guitar lesson to a third-grader, donated books

Hunter: Honors Award Committee Cochair, extended day academic support

Steward: Promoted from para-educator to full-time teacher, consistent

Introductory Letter to Staff as New Principal

A Message from Dr. Shelley McIntosh, Principal Kindergarten to Fifth Grade

It is a great honor for me to serve as the principal of the Marvin L. Winans Academy of the Performing Arts. I know you will join me in thanking the superintendent for his extraordinary leadership, and in wishing him all the best in his new position. The momentum he established will carry us through what I believe will be a straightforward transition.

Uncertainty and anxiety sometimes accompany transitions. This should not be the case for us. My highest priority is to continue to advance the core missions and vision of the Marvin L. Winans Academy of Performing Arts. I will work closely with teachers to solidify our commitment to academic and performing arts excellence. I look forward to working with our office staff and all teachers to ensure our school excels. I also intend to work closely with parents and our community in the development of shared opportunities that will benefit our students and the communities we serve.

I am asking each of you—members of our administration, faculty, and staff—to continue working with our district and Solid Rock Management Company as we move forward to fulfill our unique mission of the Marvin L. Winans Academy of Performing Arts.

∿

REFLECTION: Entering any new situation, whether it's a school or a relationship, requires an introduction of self and a glimpse into who and what of the current personnel.

∿

REFLECTION QUESTION: What are you aware of when you enter a new situation or relationship?

*I*nstruction and learning are more apt to improve when teachers have the resources they need. I believe this is the responsibility of administration, whether on a school or district level. However, in many schools, particularly in urban areas, teachers must purchase many of their instructional supplies, including pencils, paper, crayons, bulletin board items, and library books.

RESOLUTION 22

I had a degree of autonomy over budgeting and spending line items. At the beginning of the school year, each teacher was issued a $125 voucher to purchase items they needed, including bulletin board materials and wall posters. A partnership was made with a local teacher supply store where they could purchase items. Teachers could spend it all at one time or spread it over the school year as needed. Textbooks and workbooks were different line items. For furniture, such as bookcases, there was no question that a teacher needed it or not. If they requested it, teachers got it.

Money never passed through my hands. I was extremely thankful that the management company instituted that protocol. My office clerk, Mrs. Clark, was the intermediary between the principal's office and the management office regarding finances. The process involved teachers completing a supply requisition and submitting it to the office clerk. In a regularly scheduled weekly meeting with me, she presented each requisition for review and then checked it against a specific line item's balance. I approved the request by signing it. Later, the office clerk submitted the requisitions to the management company. Afterward, checks were issued for teacher supplies, which were ordered and paid for by the office clerk. When supplies arrived, she notified the teachers. Always professional, and greeting them with a friendly, dimpled smile, she eased teachers' concerns about resources.

~

REFLECTION: Systems and protocols often are perceived objectively when, in fact, they are in place to help individuals do their best.

~

REFLECTION QUESTION: Think about systems. How effective are they in supporting teachers' needs?

REALITY 23 – INSTITUTING YOGA AND MEDITATION

I was introduced to yoga in my early twenties. Since then, I have practiced yoga and meditation, written meditation stories for children, and taught yoga classes for both adults and children. Yoga and meditation not only facilitated my inner peace and well-being but also opened my chakras (energy centers), a uniquely profound experience that I will always remember. In 1975, a book authored by Deborah Rozman, *Meditating with Children*, was published and introduced to public education. At that time, it was not accepted by educational leaders even though it was grounded in research and actual experiences with children.

RESOLUTION 23

Since I experienced yoga and meditation's benefits firsthand, I met with the physical education teachers to discuss the importance of yoga stretches and students sitting quietly with a focus on their breathing. I also referred several resources. The physical education teacher viewed yoga videos and practiced movements. After her confidence and competence improved, she implemented simple yoga stretches and breathing at the end of each physical education class.

Currently, the concept of "mindfulness" has been researched and found to benefit children in classrooms. They can experience peace, calmness, and a sense of inner power. In 2008, Jai and Joy Luster launched the Calm Classroom program, including brief guided meditations and breathing exercises. It has been implemented in thousands of classrooms. As a teacher coach, I have witnessed the three-minute guided meditation being read over the public announcement system for the entire school and observing it being led by teachers in individual classrooms. Whether schools guide students via public announcement or in individual, teacher-led classrooms, the experience is what's significant. Calm Classroom exercises are only impactful if adults experience the benefits for themselves and implement exercises with a solid understanding of the connection between mind, body, and spirit. Then, Calm Classroom practices can transform students with an awareness of their value, intelligence, and power to control their own behaviors.

～

REFLECTION: I am life. My body is a universe in itself. My heart beats, my lungs breathe, my kidneys function, and my ears hear without a verbal command from me.

～

REFLECTION QUESTION: Who are you? After all titles and labels are removed, what are you aware of about yourself?

REALITY 24 – THE LITERACY DILEMMA

*B*eing able to read is a civil right, although one Michigan legislator announced that it was not. Even if a loophole in the law elicits such a response, it is a social and moral obligation to ensure that all students are literate. However, for the past thirty years, more students are not proficient in reading, and students most affected are students of color. Reviewing MEAP data and Dynamic Indicators of Basic Early Literacy Skills (DIBELS) data, most of my school students were not proficient. I asked myself why? Thus, I began my extensive research on how reading is taught in this nation. Reardon (2013) highlights the following items facing the nation:

1. A reading gap still exists between African American students when compared to Caucasian students. The same is true for Latino students.
2. Today's minority and poor student population will find it impossible to financially sustain themselves or their families if the reading gap is not effectively resolved.
3. The current dilemma facing the nation is a growing income-achievement gap.
4. The academic gap has a direct relationship on the amount of income one can earn.
5. The academic achievement gap between students from high-income and low-income families has grown significantly in the last three decades.
6. A connection exists between a low level of literacy and dropout rates and crime.
7. According to the National Adult Literacy Survey, 70% of all incarcerated adults cannot read at a fourth-grade level.

Because I taught children to read before they enrolled in kindergarten in a faith-based organization, I was confident that implementing the same Direct Instruction reading programs would increase reading proficiency in my school.

~

RESOLUTION TWENTY-FOUR

I was required by the superintendent to submit a proposal for the new reading program. Meetings were held with teachers for their input. Some voiced opposition to it being a scripted program. Although all were not supportive, I was given the approval to implement the Reading Mastery Reading Program with first-grade students. Mrs. Matt, a kindergarten teacher, requested to use Reading Mastery as a pilot for that grade; I granted her permission. We hired a direct instruction trainer and an implementation coach. With first grade teachers and one kindergarten teacher on board, we proceeded to instruct for a year. DIBELS data results identified growth in basic reading skills (phonemic awareness, letter-sound recognition, non-sense words, and fluency). Mrs. Matt's kindergarten student scores were measured higher than the other four kindergarten classrooms. With that data, plans were put into place to implement Reading Mastery and Corrective Reading school-wide.

It was a major undertaking but a necessary one. Kindergarten and first-grade teachers were trained in Reading Mastery, and second through fifth-grade teachers were trained in Corrective Reading. Teacher and student materials were purchased with grant funds. The next step was to administer placement tests that identified the level for instruction. All 700 students were tested, and only one did not need Corrective Reading support. Grade-level teams were given decision-making power as to who would teach a specific level. We were on our way to ensure our students were literate. In fact, my promise to students and parents is that children would be two or three grade levels above. I was very confident that it could be done; simply because I had already done it.

After four months into school-wide implementation, much to my dismay, I was given a directive by the superintendent to terminate the program. Being extremely disappointed is an understatement. I no longer felt that I could guarantee my promise to students and parents of reading two and three grade levels above. Pressing upon my heart was why I was parading myself as a principal, and my students aren't proficient in reading. My spirit told me to "stand still." I assured the superintendent that I would support the alternative program and the reading specialist. However, that experience continued to haunt me. I have a beautiful office and a great salary, but I have no power to teach my babies to read. Even though I thought I would retire as an administrator, I eventually decided to end my employment. I am still an advocate of direct instruction for teaching children to read. Extensive research validates my position.

∼

REFLECTION: In the midst of controversy, there can still be some compromise only if it benefits children's literacy.

∼

REFLECTION QUESTION: In what instances did you know that a program or curriculum failed to meet students' needs, and what position did you take?

*P*erception is reality. The way the principal's office is perceived influences on how teachers and staff choose to interact with the principal. I reflected on my early work experience when I was in my twenties. The workforce talk went something like this. "We don't ever see the supervisor. He comes when he wants and doesn't do the same thing we do." In reality, the supervisor's responsibilities were different, and the accusations were based on assumptions and a lack of knowledge. I have learned that assumptions tend to benefit the one doing the assuming. I believed it was my responsibility to limit assumptions.

RESOLUTION TWENTY-FIVE

To limit assumptions, I created a schedule during my first year as principal and made it accessible to the entire school staff. Note that modifications were made each new school year.

PRINCIPAL'S WEEKLY SCHEDULE – DR. MCINTOSH

Coffee with the Principal: First Monday Each Month for Parents - 7:15 a.m. to 7:45 a.m.

Time	Monday	Tuesday	Wednesday	Thursday	Friday
7:30 a.m.	Greet Students, Parent	Greet Students, Parent	Greet Students, Parent	Greet Students, Parent	Greet Students, Parent (SVSU Once a Month)
8:00 a.m.	Briefing – Administrative Assistant	Briefing – Administrative Assistant	Briefing – Administrative Assistant	Briefing – Administrative Assistant	Briefing – Administrative Assistant
10:00 a.m.	K-5 Administrative Meeting	Principals' Meeting	Open Door	Open Door	Community Alliances
11:00 a.m.	Open Door			Office Clerk	
12:30 p.m.	Lunch	Lunch	Lunch	Lunch	Lunch
1:00 p.m.	District Administrative Meeting (Bi-weekly)				
2:00 p.m.	Classroom Visits	Office Manager	Classroom Visits	Chef Meeting	Classroom Visits
3:00 p.m.	Dismissal	Dismissal	Dismissal	Dismissal	Dismissal
3:15 p.m.	Lead Teachers	K-5 Administrative Meeting	Staff Meeting	K-5 Administrative Meeting	K-5 Administrative Meeting

Schedule is subject to change due to other responsibilities associated with the Office of Principal.

Cell Phone Number: Home Phone Number:

∼

REFLECTION: The Four You(s) are:

1. Your **Front** - what you want others to see);
2. **Secret You**- what you hide from the world);
3. **Unconscious You**–the unaware you but it motivates your behavior; and,
4. **Real You**–inner divinity reflected in love, power, and intelligence.

∼

REFLECTION QUESTION: Which **YOU** is most prominent, and how does it affect your leadership?

Reality 26 – Boys and Girls Learn Differently

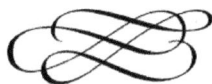

As a college professor of urban education, I taught educational psychology courses that expanded my knowledge base of how children learn and the physiological developments at different stages. For example, as students approach teenage years, their bodies are producing hormones evolving them into adults. These changes affect their moods. They may be easily irritated or act out impulsively. In addition, students' awareness of their changing bodies may also adversely affect behaviors and learning in the classroom. I posed the question, "How can we best support our fifth graders who are approaching teenage years?" The administrative team, by consensus, recommended that teaching staff participate in a book study of *How Boys and Girls Learn Differently* by Michael Gurian.

Resolution Twenty-Six

Copies of *How Boys and Girls Learn Differently* were purchased for the staff. Assigned chapters were read and discussed in small groups during faculty meetings, with a PowerPoint Presentation identifying some key characteristics that were discussed. These included the following: Girls have, in general, stronger neural connectors in their temporal lobes than boys have. These connectors lead to more sensory detailed memory storage, better listening skills, and better discrimination among various voice tones. This leads, among other things, to greater use of detail in writing assignments. Girls' prefrontal cortex is generally more active than boys' and develops at earlier ages.

For this reason, girls tend to make fewer impulsive decisions than boys do. Further, girls have more serotonin in the bloodstream and the brain, making them biochemically less impulsive. Because boys' brains have more cortical areas dedicated to spatial-mechanical functioning, males use, on average, half the brain space that females use for verbal-emotive functioning. The cortical trend toward spatial-mechanical functioning makes many boys want to move objects through space, like balls, model airplanes, or just their arms and legs. Most boys, although not all of them, will experience words and feelings differently than girls do (Blum, 1997; Moir & Jessel, 1989). The male brain is set to renew, recharge, and reorient itself by entering what neurologists call a *rest state*. The boy in the back of the classroom whose eyes are drifting toward sleep has entered a neural rest state. It is predominantly boys who drift off without completing assignments, who stop taking notes and fall asleep during a lecture, or who tap pencils or otherwise fidget in hopes of keeping themselves awake and learning. Females tend to recharge and reorient neural focus without rest states. Thus, a girl can be bored with a lesson, but she will nonetheless keep her eyes open, take notes, and perform relatively well. This is especially true when the teacher uses more words to teach a lesson instead of being spatial and diagrammatic. The more words a teacher uses, the more likely boys are to "zone out" or go into a rest state. The male brain is better suited for symbols, abstractions, diagrams, pictures, and objects moving through space than for the monotony of words (Educational Leadership, 2004 Volume 62, Number 3 Pages 21-26 Gurian & Stevens, 2004).

The plan was to set up gender-specific classrooms as a pilot for the fifth grade. A female and a male teacher were needed with a preference for teachers currently teaching the fifth grade. We were happy that two teachers were willing to teach in gender-specific classrooms. Each teacher had the freedom to design their classrooms with boys and girls in mind. The boys' classroom was adorned with posters of African American athletes, engineers, and scientists. The color design was brown and beige. Brown bean bags and a couple of basketballs were part of the reading corner. The girls' classroom color was purple, depicting royalty. In fact, they referred to themselves as princesses. Bean bags, bulletin boards, and table covers were all purple. Both teachers selected specific strategies that support optimal learning of each gender.

When I visited both classrooms, I noticed a sense of calmness and positive interactions among the students. Tendencies of girls to compete for boys' attention and boys showing off for girls were absent. The girls were asking questions freely and engaging in discussions. Similarly, this occurred with the boys. However, project-based, competitive, and inquiry-driven instruction would have served the boys even better in retrospect. Overall, the learning in both classrooms improved.

～

REFLECTION: Embedded in each boy and girl's DNA is the potential to evolve into men and women. Though magical, it requires adults' knowledge and understanding of how this growth affects their mood, behaviors, and learning.

～

REFLECTION QUESTION: Recall a memory of being an adolescent; what do you wish adults, teachers, or parents understood about you?

When students know their own people's history, it enlightens them with a sense of pride and purpose. When they see principals and teachers that look like them in the same vein, they feel a sense of kinship and belonging. However, these are predicated upon positive interactions between staff and students. Most textbooks fail to tell the story of the contributions of Chinese, Japanese, Native Americans, and African Americans to the world and to building America. In addition, many have minimal cultural knowledge of each of these groups. Without historical and cultural knowledge, teachers and administrators are at a disadvantage in offering the most effective guidance and instruction.

RESOLUTION TWENTY-SEVEN

One way I addressed this was to show a video entitled the *Real Eve* at a faculty meeting as an introduction to Black History Month. In fact, this resource was provided by my art teacher. The video scientifically traced the origin of the human race to an African woman. Needless to say, this touched the nerves of some teachers because it contradicted their knowledge and beliefs. I did state a disclaimer regarding the video supported evolution. A couple of courageous teachers wanted to meet with me for discussion, which I did. I answered their questions with the hope it would expand their knowledge. The video was a springboard to the initiative for Black History Month. That initiative required that all classrooms adopt an African country, study its history and culture, and reorganize the classroom to reflect these. At the end of the month, the administrative team and I toured each classroom, shared observations with faculty, and awarded the best room. As always, most teachers committed themselves to the initiative, while a few gave it minimal effort.

Another way to address this reality was to discuss what culturally responsive teaching is. The information below was presented in a faculty meeting and a handout distributed to each teacher.

Culturally Responsive Teaching Is Validating

Gay (2000) defines culturally responsive teaching as using the cultural knowledge, prior experiences, and performance styles of diverse students to make learning more appropriate and effective for them; it teaches to and through these students' strengths. Gay (2000) also describes culturally responsive teaching as having these characteristics:

- It acknowledges the legitimacy of different ethnic groups' cultural heritage, both as legacies that affect students' dispositions, attitudes, and approaches to learning and as worthy content to be taught in the formal curriculum.
- It builds bridges of meaningfulness between home and school experiences and between academic abstractions and lived sociocultural realities.
- It uses a wide variety of instructional strategies that are connected to different learning styles.
- It teaches students to know and praise their own and each others' cultural heritage.
- It incorporates multicultural information, resources, and materials in all the subjects and skills routinely taught in schools.

Using these characteristics to improve culturally responsive teaching would involve considerations to the classroom environment. Literature in the classroom would reflect multiple ethnic perspectives and literary genres. Math instruction would incorporate everyday-life concepts, such as economics, employment, consumer habits, of various ethnic groups. To teach to students' different learning styles, activities would reflect a variety of sensory opportunities: visual, auditory, tactile (Gay, 2000).

Culturally responsive teaching was included as a component of the Highly Effective Instruction Observation Tool used by the principal and assistant principal in teacher walk-throughs. See Figure 1.

Characteristics	1st Date: Subject:	2nd Date: Subject:	3rd Date: Subject:	4th Date: Subject:
1. Engaged Students: Active in Learning Process				
a. Problem-Solving Group Work				
b. Effective Questioning				
c. Role Playing				
d. Visual Discovery				
e. Social Studies Skills Builders (map reading, community building, civic responsibility)				
f. Writing for Understanding				
2. Posted Learning Standards / Objectives Written in Student Language				
3. Teacher Involvement in Learning (What is the teacher doing?)				
a. Modeling				
b. Mini-Lessons				
c. Lecturing (Teacher-Directed)				
d. Positive Interaction with students				
e. Re-teaching				
f. Monitoring				
4. Technology Use in Learning Process				
5. Walk the Walls: Evidence of student work / Evidence of vocabulary building				
6. Stimulating Environment				
a. Creative, relevant bulletin boards				
b. Maps, globes				
c. Visuals, pictures, portraits				
d. Timelines of historical events				
e. Math manipulatives, calculators (accessible)				
7. Centers				
8. Culturally Relevant Materials				
a. Transparencies-diverse cultures				
b. Literature/fiction & non-fiction diversity				
c. Videos				
d. Newspapers, magazines				
e. Cultural artifacts (pictures, actual clothing, instruments, diets)				
f. Music (tapes, CDs)				
9. Classroom Expectations, Behavior Norms				
a. Management system / routines				
b. Rules posted				
c. Reinforcement of appropriate behaviors / praise / compliments				
d. Redirection of inappropriate behaviors				

Comments:

Administrator Signature:

_____

≈

REFLECTION: We all belong to the human race yet to a certain ethnic or "racial" group. Having knowledge and pride of our own should open us to the value of others that are different.

≈

REFLECTION QUESTION: Recall your education in elementary, middle, or high school; how much did you learn about the contributions of people of color, such as African Americans, Hispanics, Native Americans, and Asian Americans?

EPILOGUE

The nurturing of my competence, autonomy, and relatedness was through supportive environments. Some of these include:

My mother and father providing basic needs of food, shelter, and clothing. My father walking his three daughters to the neighborhood library, where I acquired a love for reading.

My kindergarten teacher taught me how to hold my pencil correctly and write letters with so much practice that a callous formed on my index finger.

Mr. Dixon, my eighth-grade typing teacher, told the class to learn the home keys on the typewriter. We didn't. So, he covered all the keys on thirty manual typewriters with tape. We asked, "What happened?" He answered, "I told you to learn the home keys." Then, he demonstrated that he could type 100 words in one minute by knowing the home keys. I learned that keyboard and still apply it in my work today.

The computer lab assistant while I was in undergrad, as a grown adult, could see my despair in not completing a Word document, a database, and a graphic. Everyone had completed the assignments and left. He looked at me and asked, "What's wrong?" Tears flowing, I told him I don't even know how to turn on the computer. Pulling up a chair, he sat next to me and said, "Don't worry. I will sit with you as long as it takes and teach you."

The late Reverend Albert B. Cleage, founder of the Shrines of the Black Madonna, told young people, "You are leaders," and required disciplined study initially by reading approximately fifteen books so we could understand African history, the status of Black people in America, unequal laws and practices, and the oppressive system in which we live; thus, inspiring us to build a better world—a counter system.

"You can't see the forest for the trees." These experiences, metaphorically speaking, were my forest, the encouraging environment that nurtured intrinsic motivation. For urban school principals, the following are very helpful in creating an encouraging environment.

Self-Awareness: Conscious knowledge of one's own character, feelings, motives, and desires.

Empathy: The ability to understand and share the feelings of another.

Team Building: The process of causing a group of people to work together to increase motivation and promote cooperation.

Literacy: Teach students to read *The World and The Word* by Joan Wink. In reading that book, students understand the system in which they live and that poverty is created just as wealth is. The reality of their conditions, oppressed and exploited, must be critically analyzed so the mantra could be, we seek to end our oppression. Remind students daily of the contributions that are being made today by their people and others. In reading the *Word*, the use of direct instruction to teach letter-sound recognition, sounding out, and blending is most effective. Teach concepts through visual images, demonstrations, role-playing, and student discussions.

∽

Final Reflection

Our lives are interwoven, even though we are different. We encourage, uplift, and support students, teachers, and parents. For each decision and deed, we ask: Am I leading in such a way that my acts create an environment that recognizes and nurture competence, autonomy, and relatedness for all those in the school community? We desire to answer with a resounding YES!

I'm from student assemblies

Teachers calling parents for summer school

From fifth grade trips to Washington, DC

From cheerleaders cute and cool

From teachers dressed like Little Red Robin Hood

From school-wide cleanup, Zoom, Zip, and Zap

And from children behaving as they should!

From waking up daily at 5 o'clock,

A.M. that is.

And putting on mismatched shoes in the dark,

Glad I noticed.

Being inundated with many tasks,

I rush into my own office and ask

my admin team

Has anyone seen Doctor McIntosh?

Oh, that's me!

I'm from education chose me.

ALSO BY SHELLEY MCINTOSH ED.D

A Principal's Tale: Life In 31 Days

Mtoto House: Vision to Victory: Raising African American Children Communally

Genesis II: The Re-Creation of Black People

www.ingramcontent.com/pod-product-compliance
Lightning Source LLC
Chambersburg PA
CBHW060243030426
42335CB00014B/1579